Winning with Your Body, Mind, and Soul

Winning with Your Body, Mind, and Soul

Going All In

HENRY ARNOLD DAVIS

RESOURCE *Publications* · Eugene, Oregon

WINNING WITH YOUR BODY, MIND, AND SOUL
Going All In

Copyright © 2024 Davis, Henry Arnold. All rights reserved. Except for brief quotations in critical publications or reviews, no part of this book may be reproduced in any manner without prior written permission from the publisher. Write: Permissions, Wipf and Stock Publishers, 199 W. 8th Ave., Suite 3, Eugene, OR 97401.

Resource Publications
An Imprint of Wipf and Stock Publishers
199 W. 8th Ave., Suite 3
Eugene, OR 97401

www.wipfandstock.com

PAPERBACK ISBN: 979-8-3852-1801-1
HARDCOVER ISBN: 979-8-3852-1802-8
EBOOK ISBN: 979-8-3852-1803-5

Unless otherwise indicated, all Scripture quotations are taken from the Holy Bible, New Living Translation, copyright © 1996, 2004, 2007, 2013, 2015 by Tyndale House Foundation. Used by permission of Tyndale House Publishers, Inc., Carol Stream, Illinois 60188. All rights reserved.

Where indicated, Scripture quotations taken from the Amplified® Bible Classic, Copyright © 1954, 1958, 1962, 1964, 1965, 1987 by The Lockman Foundation. Used by permission. (www.Lockman.org)

Where indicated, Scripture quotations from The Authorized (King James) Version. Rights in the Authorized Version in the United Kingdom are vested in the Crown. Reproduced by permission of the Crown's patentee, Cambridge University Press.

Where indicated, Scripture taken from the HOLY BIBLE, NEW INTERNATIONAL VERSION. Copyright © 1973, 1978, 1984 International Bible Society. Used by permission of Zondervan Bible Publishers.

Where indicated, Scripture taken from the New King James Version®. Copyright © 1982 by Thomas Nelson. Used by permission. All rights reserved.

Partial lyric reprint of Anne Wilson, Jeff Pardo, and Matthew West, "My Jesus," Jacobs Story Music (BMI) Brenthood Music (BMI) Meaux Mercy (BMI) Capitol CMG Paragon (BMI), 2021. All rights reserved. Used by permission.

"Decision-Making Process," https://www.umassd.edu/fycm/decision-making/process/. Used by permission of Daryl Poeira, Director of Web Systems and Communications, University Marketing at UMass Dartmouth.

Excerpt from Alzheimer's Association. "Alzheimer's Disease: Facts and Figures." 2024. https://www.alz.org/alzheimers-dementia/facts-figures. Used by permission of the Alzheimer's Association.

Excerpt from BBC. "Modern Spiritualism: Beliefs." Religions, last updated Sept. 9, 2009. http://www.bbc.co.uk/religion/religions/spiritualism/beliefs/beliefs_1.shtml. Used by permission of the BBC.

Excerpt from BBC. "Jainism: The Soul." Religions, last updated Sept. 10, 2009. http://www.bbc.co.uk/religion/religions/jainism/beliefs/soul.shtml. Used by permission of the BBC.

Excert from Humanists UK. "Non-religious Beliefs." https://humanists.uk/humanism/humanism-today/non-religious-beliefs/. Used by permission of Humanists UK.

Dedicated to Eddie Lee Davis—Dee La,
who taught me how to win and to Charlene Winston-Puryear—
my second mom, who gave me the love of my life.

Before reading this book, I highly recommend you read
Gambling With Your Soul: What Is Your Best Bet?

Go to the end of this book ("Other Titles from Henry Arnold Davis") to see what readers are saying about
Gambling With Your Soul.

Table of Contents

Illustrations and Tables x
Acknowledgments xi
Introduction xv

PART I: Winning with Your Body

    Chapter 1: The Start 3
    Chapter 2: The Work 9
    Chapter 3: The Finish 22

PART II: Winning with Your Mind

    Chapter 4: Mind over Matter 31
    Chapter 5: Mind Games 37

PART III: Winning with Your Soul

    Chapter 6: Forgiveness 47
    Chapter 7: Finding Desire 52
    Chapter 8: Forging Ability 81

Conclusion 101
Bibliography 111
Appendix A: Major Religions of the World 117
Appendix B: Afterlife Beliefs 120
Appendix C: Probability of Achieving Your Desire with Each Major Religion 152
About the Author 164
Other Titles from Henry Arnold Davis 165

Illustrations and Tables

1. Probability of Achieving the Desired Afterlife, Summarized (Chapter 7)
2. Probability of Achieving Your Desire with Each Major Religion: 1–4 (Appendix C)
3. Probability of Achieving Your Desire with Each Major Religion: 5–6 (Appendix C)
4. Probability of Achieving Your Desire with Each Major Religion: 7 (Appendix C)
5. Probability of Achieving Your Desire with Each Major Religion: 8–12 (Appendix C)
6. Probability of Achieving Your Desire with Each Major Religion: 13–17 (Appendix C)
7. Probability of Achieving Your Desire with Each Major Religion: 18–22 (Appendix C)

Acknowledgments

To MY SWEET WIFE, lifelong partner, and biggest fan, Tanya, for her encouragement and unwavering support during the writing of this book, from before the first words made their way to the blank page. You are my inspiration, the first sight to start my day and the last voice in my ear every night. Thanks for embarking on this journey with me and your tireless efforts, thoughtful edits, and well-timed "Is it done yet?" which kept the ink flowing.

To my generous and loving big sister, Deborah Davis-Leicht, with a smile as bright as the morning sun, an insane amount of energy, and an all-consuming beautiful spirit: thank you for providing the opportunity that laid the book's foundation—before the idea was even formed.

To my big sister, author, and songwriter, Joyce Tines, who connected the dots and provided the right perspective to weave some vital strands together: thanks for your fine tuning and for allowing the book to stay true to its intent.

To my powerful, spirit-filled little brother and kingdom-building warrior, Marvin Davis, with a hope as deep as the ocean, a heart as big as the Montana sky, and an unshakable love for humanity: thank you for lifting the book to new heights.

To my courageous, determined big brother and confidant, Ran Davis, who provided invaluable feedback on the beginnings of the manuscript: thanks for your keen insight, which set the book's overarching message on a clear trajectory.

To my fellow Eli and miracle-minded executive coach, David C. Asomaning, whose focus is more pointed than the tip of any spear: thanks for your sage advice, probing questions, dedication, and unparalleled passion in driving this work to be the best it could be.

Acknowledgments

To my fellow writer and unofficial editor, Priscilla H. Douglas, who was able to see the big picture as well as the fine detail: thank you for providing the perfect balance of critique and criticism to ensure all i's were dotted, t's crossed, and ideas fully connected.

To my friend, faith-filled sister, and Memphis transplant, Nadja Fidelia, who helped expand the team's support structure in ways that cannot be measured: thanks for your incredible resourcefulness and generosity, which always brought together the right complement of skills, tools, and personnel to knock down any roadblock the team encountered.

To my friend, former crewmate, and stroke from the land Down Under, Andrew Fletcher, whose unique perspective and vantage point are cherished: thanks for sharing your thoughts, commentary, and analysis on winning—the thrilling, magical, elusive, demanding, and often unpredictable nature of it.

To my friend, former crewmate, and fearless captain, James "Jamie" Henry Edmondson Fosburgh, whose insights, recollections, and authenticity are priceless: thanks for filling in some irreplaceable details that will enrich the reader's experience with our treasured story.

To my friend, former classmate, and fellow laborer in the kingdom, Paula Fuller, whose dedication, sincerity, and generosity is endless: thanks for being an incredible listener, a tremendous springboard, and an active supporter in sharing your inspiring network, which made the book richer and fuller.

To my friend, former roommate, and legal eagle, Lucas Torres, who provided the perfect balance of critique and criticism: thanks for sharing your sharp mind, sharp pencil, and invaluable perspective, which will without question expand the book's reach.

To my former high school guidance counselors and staunch advocates, Martha "Marty" Watkins and Glenda Cryer, who served as foundational pillars in the lives of so many students: thanks for setting my feet on a path of knowledge that led to new horizons full of wisdom and understanding.

To all the members of the Yale crew family who were intricate and invaluable partners in rounding out a vital part of the story: the book is made whole from your contributions. Special thanks to Andrew Card—Y150 alumni head coach of lightweight crew, Michael Hard—member of the Yale Crew Association Board of Directors, and Thomas Weil—preeminent and self-appointed Yale crew historian, for your remarkable resourcefulness and unselfishness.

Acknowledgments

To my inspiring coach, H. Richter Elser, and awesome crewmates—Jamie Fosburgh, Charles Gately, Christopher Ozburn, Jonathan Leone, Ramsey Walker, Stephen Riley, David Weyerhaeuser, and William Mc-Glashan—from the 1983 undefeated lightweight first freshman boat, the EARC Eastern Sprints champions who went all in—every minute, second, fraction of a second when the moment called for it—and carved our place in rowing history. Thank you for sharing your passions, thoughts, and experiences—the finger that pulled the trigger and launched this work into motion.

Introduction

SHORTLY AFTER THE PUBLICATION of my first book, *Gambling With Your Soul: What Is Your Best Bet?*, I was invited to give a talk, to take part in a webinar series by NMA… *the* leadership development organization. It was originally named the Foreman's Club of Dayton then, later, The National Management Association. As the name suggests, the organization focuses on leadership.

My first thought was, What can I possibly add to this topic? Or should I say this "art," as Max DePree described it in *Leadership Is an Art*. There have probably been more books written on leadership than on any other subject. Entire careers—of writers, consultants, life coaches, motivational speakers, etc.—and industries have been built upon it. And no wonder: Leadership cuts across every dimension of our human experience. It touches all aspects of our personal and professional lives—from our most private, intimate moments to those actions on public display for all the world to see, from the beginning until the end of our lives.

Regardless of the activity or pursuit, leadership is a critical component in the amount of success achieved. Whether we are engaged in an activity involving only ourselves or one with a group, being a good leader is essential. Leaders know how to lead themselves to the winner's circle, as well as take a group—a family, team, battalion, organization, congregation, country—there. In fact, John C. Maxwell has put in plain language in his *The 21 Irrefutable Laws of Leadership* the rules we can follow to success. And Priscilla H. Douglas tells us in her *Woke Leadership* that the best of the best operate within a woke leadership model. These leaders are able to get the best performance from all those involved—starting with themselves. They lead with purpose, conviction, and compassion.

Now certainly success is relative to everyone and based on their unique, specific goal. A runner can be successful with an eight-minute mile

Introduction

if that was her goal. She does not have to take home the gold medal at the Olympics to be a winner. So, what does it take to be a winner?

A Google search with Oxford Languages defines a win as "a successful result in a contest, conflict, bet, or other endeavor; a victory."[1] From the definition, first and foremost, we must determine what constitutes "a successful result." In other words, What does winning look like? And to be more exact, What does it look like for each of us individually?

In the above example with the runner, coming in first place at the world's premiere sporting competition may not have been her criteria for a successful result. It was not her definition of what is required to be a winner. And that is perfectly fine. Setting realistic goals is a fundamental step in the process. Then adjusting our expectations and emotional responses to the attainment, or lack thereof, of those goals is paramount. Often, happiness is tied to our ability to be successful—in other words, to win—with a particular goal or more generally, in life altogether. And on the flip side, sadness, or disappointment, which causes us to feel like a loser, is directly tied to not achieving success with the goals we set for ourselves.

However, not all goals we strive to achieve are set by ourselves. Sadly, more often than we care to admit, our goals are set by someone else. We subconsciously adopt them as if they were created by us. And that is okay if the goals align with our values and overall plan for our lives. But when they do not, it causes us unwanted stress and anxiety.

How many times have we heard a parent say their child is going to be a star athlete with an amazing professional career? Words uttered before the child is even born. Or their child is going to take over the family business once they retire? Never mind the child has been gifted in a completely different area and has no interest in running the family business. What about the corporate executive, coach, or commander who sets a goal and fails to get buy-in from the team responsible for executing it? But to be good soldiers, the team marches forward.

When these situations occur, they cause us to question why we do the things we do and ultimately the meaning of life—or at a minimum, the meaning of our lives. This calibration process is never-ending, tuned continuously over our lifetimes. We will revisit this dynamic throughout the book.

It has been said that winning is all about attitude. You may be familiar with the expression "Your attitude determines your altitude." For sure,

---

1. *Oxford Languages*, "Win."

Introduction

having a positive attitude is always a good thing. But is a good attitude necessary to be a winner?

Whether you are a tennis fan or not, you probably recognize the name John McEnroe. Wikipedia describes him as "an American former professional tennis player. He was known for his shot-making and volleying skills, in addition to confrontational on-court behavior that frequently landed him in trouble with umpires and tennis authorities. McEnroe attained the world No. 1 ranking in both singles and doubles, finishing his career with 77 singles and 78 doubles titles; this remains the highest men's combined total of the Open Era."[2] He is one of the most decorated players in the history of the sport. So, I gather winning does not require a good attitude.

When was the last time you were told that you can do anything you put your mind to? It must be something taught in Parenting 101 and to all the village elders. Well, at five-feet, six-inches tall—and lacking the vertical leaping abilities of Michael Anthony Jerome "Spud" Webb—I will not be winning any Slam Dunk Contests—no matter how much I put my mind to it.

Many people associate winning with just being lucky. Certainly, luck plays a part in many ventures and areas of our lives—a larger part in some lives. But to be a consistent winner, Eliyahu M. Goldratt assures us in *It's Not Luck* that winning is not due to luck. Stephen R. Covey has identified, in *The 7 Habits of Highly Effective People*, seven habits that, when practiced with discipline and refined over time, forge into skills and turn out winners.

My talk was entitled "The DNA of a Winner." Winning can be an elusive thing. Anyone who has chased a dream can relate. We see others achieve the goals we have set for ourselves and wonder, Why can't I fix that one thing that is holding me back? Shave two seconds off my time. Sink 5 percent more free-throws. Stay focused on creative solutions when confronted with difficult personalities. Find that missing piece of evidence to solve the case. Say just the right thing at just the right moment to close the deal.

Depending on the specific activity, winning can involve a multitude of factors. Some are within our control. Some are outside our control. However, regardless of the activity, there are two foundational elements present inside of every winner: desire and ability.

Another Google search with Oxford Languages defines desire as "a strong feeling of wanting to have something or wishing for something to

---

2. Wikipedia, "John McEnroe."

Introduction

happen."[3] This is the first building block. And to determine the strength of this block, we must test it. Does the thought of achieving it energize us? Does it force us to act? Do we anticipate a satisfying emotional response to achieving it? If the answer to each of these questions is not a resounding yes, then it is not the type of desire we are looking for. It needs to be something that moves us to action. We cannot sit still. We cannot be silent. We cannot accept the status quo. There is a hunger—beyond the physical need for food—that must be satisfied, a thirst that must be quenched. Our heart, mind, and soul will not rest until we have it.

Along with a burning desire, all winners have ability. Naturally, all human beings have some degree of talent in just about every area. However, every talent does not make its way into an ability. Roy L. Smith asserts that "discipline is the refining fire by which talent becomes ability." Merriam-Webster defines ability as "the quality or state of being able; especially the physical, mental, or legal power to do something." And I will add, to do something—whatever "something" is—better than most people. Research has concluded that a human being's ability in six areas—attention, creativity, flexibility, focus, memory, and speed—directly affects the amount of success the person will ultimately enjoy.

And every person with a particular ability is not a winner. To be a winner, a person must merge desire and ability, find the overlap. That narrow strip where their heart, mind, and soul will not rest, and their skill/ability—polished into a sparkling jewel with dogged determination—intersect. The sweet spot: this is where winners live.

So, the million-dollar question is, How do we find the sweet spot? We find it by listening—carefully, completely—to ourselves as well as to others. And, by using more than our ears.

To find desire, we start by recognizing and accepting our basic human needs. Renowned psychologist Abraham Harold Maslow theorized that all human beings have five levels of needs that must be satisfied for a person to reach her full potential. Late in his life, he added a sixth level: self-transcendence. He placed them in a hierarchy from the lowest to the highest. But he also emphasized that the hierarchy is not as rigidly fixed an order as it is often presented:

- Level 1: Physical Survival Needs (Survival Instinct)
- Level 2: Physical Safety Needs (Survival Instinct)

3. *Oxford Languages*, "Desire."

Introduction

- Level 3: Love and Belonging Needs
- Level 4: Self-Esteem Needs
- Level 5: Self-Fulfilled/Self-Actualized Needs
- Level 6: Self-Transcendence Needs (Self-Preservation Instinct)

For most of his life, Maslow maintained, as do many religions/non-religions, that self-actualization—a term coined by the organismic theorist Kurt Goldstein[4]—is the ultimate desire of every human being. As mentioned above, late in his life Maslow added self-transcendence but was unable to fully develop it due to his untimely death. He believed that this level 6 need was the pinnacle desire of all human beings. We will revisit this most important, supreme need later in our discussion. Either consciously or subconsciously, we want to be all that we can be—to be complete. And most of the learning here comes from looking inward.

To find ability, most of the learning comes from looking outward, by seeking feedback from others on their perception of our performance. This comes in various forms: There are results that can be readily assessed from direct competition with others, including athletic competitions, artistic displays, verbal debates, mentally challenging games, and the like. They provide statistics to slice and dice for head-to-head comparisons on any dimension. We can also determine ability from the success of our creations—art, music, film, book, automobile, aircraft, computer, software, building, etc. Again, with all the necessary statistics—sales, market share, profitability, ranking, etc.—we can determine objectively where we stand in relation to others. Or knowledge can be gained indirectly or subjectively, with less defined methods of assessment. But this is no less important. Our ability to inspire others, diffuse a situation, or navigate around land mines provides invaluable information about our skills.

Picture the Chinese symbol for yin and yang with its dark and light teardrops forming a complete circle. Draw a vertical line down the center. Yin-dark is on the right and yang-light is on the left—however, not entirely. A portion of each teardrop is present in both halves of the circle. The right side depicts the type of listening required to find our desire: 80 percent to ourselves, 20 percent to others. The left side depicts the type of listening required to find our ability: 80 percent to others, 20 percent to ourselves.

---

4. Wikipedia, "Self-Actualization."

Introduction

Now, to complete levels 5 and 6 and become self-fulfilled/self-actualized and then achieve self-transcendence, that is to win as a human being; we must find the sweet spot. And we do that by merging desire and ability for our whole selves, all three components: body, mind, and soul—separately and collectively.

In part I, we explore what it takes to win with our bodies. In doing so, we confirm the formidable linkage between the body and the mind: sometimes magical, always mystical. One of the most difficult concepts to explain is the basic connection and interdependence of the body, specifically the physical brain and the mind. It is known as the mind-body problem.

Throughout history some of the most intelligent humans to walk the planet have studied the mind. Important philosophers of mind include Plato, Patanjali, René Descartes, Gottfried Wilhelm Leibniz, John Locke, George Berkeley—known as Bishop Berkeley (bishop of Cloyne)—David Hume, Immanuel Kant, G. W. F. Hegel, Arthur Schopenhauer, John Searle, Daniel Dennett, Jerry Fodor, Thomas Nagel, and David Chalmers. The description and definition of the mind is also a part of psychology. Esteemed psychologists Sigmund Freud and William James have developed influential theories about the nature of the mind. And renowned computer scientists have also studied the mind. Alan Mathison Turing and Hilary Whitehall Putnam devoted significant time to develop impactful theories about the mind's makeup and operation.[5] Yet the mind remains one of the greatest mysteries of a human being.

In part II, we probe the mind to reveal its near limitless—and often untapped—power. We discover how harnessing it can take us to the winner's circle—every single time.

In our investigation, we consider the mind from the perspective of monism as well as dualism. Most modern philosophers of mind (including Jerry Fodor, Daniel Dennett, and Hilary Putnam) maintain, albeit in different ways, that the mind is not something separate from the body.[6] This is in line with the position advanced by monism. From either a physicalist (also referred to as a materialist) or an idealist perspective, the mind and brain are considered one and the same, be it all physical or all mental. There is only one entity.

Dualism is the concept that the mind and the body, specifically the brain, are two distinct and separate things. They have a material and a

---

5. Wikipedia, "Mind."
6. Wikipedia, "Mind-Body Problem."

Introduction

nonmaterial component. The brain is a physical or material substance that can be touched, measured, weighed, and viewed with the naked eye. It is governed by physics and mathematics within our universe and impacted by its natural laws and forces. All dualists accept this narrative of the brain. The narrative of the mind, however, is divided between two groups: substance dualists and property dualists.

For a dualist, the mind is either an independently existing substance of a nonmaterial nature or a group of independent nonphysical mental properties. It has a spiritual dimension that includes consciousness and the basis for thoughts, memories, the ability to reason, and the like. It is not subject to the physical laws of our universe. You cannot touch it, measure it, weigh it, or see it. The mind manifests itself through the brain the way sound waves manifest themselves through a radio. We enjoy the melodies being projected by the radio, but the music is not part of the radio.

It is important to note that the word mind is often used interchangeably with the words spirit or soul by dualists and by monists categorized as idealists. Thus, when discussing the components (body, mind, and soul) of a human being, mind and soul are generally lumped together, giving a human being only two components. In this makeup of a human being, there is agreement that the mind/soul/spirit survives death—the physical destruction of the body. For our discussion, we will use three components (body, mind, and soul) to represent a human being. This construct aligns more directly with the perspective of monists categorized as physicalists as well as the perspective of most modern philosophers. And in this makeup of a human being, there is agreement that the mind, but not the soul, is destroyed when the physical body is destroyed. So, in either view of a human being (two components or three components), the soul remains after physical death.

And lastly, in part III, we unveil what it takes to win with our soul. We pull back the curtain to find the definition of a successful result for the soul (or spirit, mind, consciousness, energy, force, etc.—whatever you call that part of a human being which survives physical death). And we answer the question, What does a win look like for our soul? But more importantly, How do we achieve it? And if human beings do not have a soul, or anything else that continues beyond physical death, we address that perspective as well.

So, let's start.

PART I: WINNING WITH YOUR BODY

> The Word became flesh and made his dwelling among us. We have seen his glory, the glory of the one and only Son, who came from the Father, full of grace and truth.
>
> —John 1:14 (NIV)

Chapter 1: The Start

"You don't have to be great to start, but you have to start to be great."
—Zig Ziglar

"At the end of the day, you are solely responsible for your success and your failure. And the sooner you realize that, you accept that, and integrate that into your work ethic, you will start being successful. As long as you blame others for the reason you aren't where you want to be, you will always be a failure."
—Erin Cummins

"Start by doing what's necessary; then do what's possible; and suddenly you are doing the impossible."
—Francis of Assisi

Kapow! As it had done since 1960, the starter's gun at Regatta Point on Lake Quinsigamond told the oarsmen it is time to race. Without that familiar sound, their bodies would remain in the "ready" position. Backs upright, leaning slightly forward. Legs bent at the knees, forming an upside-down *V* nestled into their chests. And arms outstretched, holding the oar's handle with a firm grip. At the catch. Every muscle in their bodies taut. Yet relaxed. Like a lion about to pounce on its prey. Or the sprinter in her starter blocks, ready to be shot out of a cannon. Spring-loaded. Eyes straight ahead. They have been taught not to look outside of the boat. That is the coxswain's job. To win, all eight rowers must act as one. And to act as one, they must focus all their attention on doing exactly—not something close to, but exactly—what their teammate in front of them is doing.

Spectators lined the banks of the lake. The largest crowds, at the finish and starting lines. The spring sun was welcomed with outstretched arms. Shaking off the last signs of a stubborn grey winter, people relished the opportunity to breakout their less-concealing wardrobe—sleeveless dresses, tank tops, T-shirts, shorts, skirts, skorts, open-toed shoes, straw hats. The sunlight raced across the face of the calm waters. And the vibrant colors created a delightful rainbow as I looked back at the shore from the coxswain's seat. Ah, the smell of spring was in the air.

For rowing enthusiasts, the 1983 regular season for the eighteen schools in the Eastern Association of Rowing Colleges (EARC) had been nothing short of spectacular. In the men's lightweight varsity category, Princeton was undefeated and the number one seed. Yale was number two with their only loss to Princeton. In the men's lightweight freshman category, Yale was undefeated and the number one seed. Dartmouth was number two with their only loss to Yale. All four boats were poised for a rematch, and the crowds were just as excited to witness it. The atmosphere was electric. Even sitting several hundred yards away from the crowds out on the water, I could feel their energy—not to mention the tightrope tension within the boat. We could not wait to get it on.

The 1983 EARC Eastern Sprints in Worcester, Massachusetts began like a hundred other races for the Yale lightweight first freshman boat—the "First Frosh." Half. Three-quarters. Half. Full. These are the lengths of strokes taken to get the boat up out of the water and quickly build momentum. With eight oarsmen averaging one hundred and fifty pounds and a coxswain, with supplemental sandbags if necessary, weighing at least one hundred and twenty-five pounds, that is a lot of weight to get moving from a dead start. This routine is one of the most practiced drills for race preparation. In crew, like most sporting events, the start of the competition is vital. Your position relative to the other boats determines whether the team—and by team, I mean the stroke and the coxswain—stays with your pre-race strategy or changes it on the fly.

"Settle." That is the command uttered by the coxswain after a set number of full strokes, usually ten, after the partial strokes. The boat drops into its race cadence. Although we had recently raced at a higher rate, our typical rate was around thirty-four strokes per minute. After countless hours on the water in numerous scenarios—practice, seat-racing, sprints, long rows, short rows, races, etc.—it was the rate determined by the coach, stroke, and

Chapter 1: The Start

coxswain that worked best for the eight guys in the boat today, and for the specific race at hand.

With an undefeated season and winning our heat that morning, Yale's First Frosh had one of the best positional lane assignments—lane three—for the championship race. Its starboard boundary formed the centerline of the six-boat competition. From here it was easy to see our position after the start. We were known for a fast start, and rarely—if ever—did we find ourselves behind another boat coming off the starting line. In crew, you want to be in front to take advantage of the smooth water, if there is any. And thankfully, today's weather conditions would offer it to the fastest crew. With mild winds—about seven to ten miles per hour, clear skies with over seven miles of visibility, and a maximum temperature of seventy degrees Fahrenheit—it was a perfect day for racing.

Once the boat in front of you disturbs the water, it creates ripples or a wake. This adds more drag on your boat, slowing you down. To overcome the additional resistance, the rowers must burn more energy—both mentally and physically. More mental focus is required to keep the boat level, to raise and lower the oars with precise timing, and to sense the body movements of your fellow rowers. More physical exertion is needed to muscle through the rougher water, to pull the oars out of the water, and oftentimes to take more strokes per minute for longer periods of time. All these things cause your rowers to tire out faster. Now in a sprint or side-by-side race, where each boat has its own lane, there is less impact on the trailing boat than in a head style race. But nonetheless, you do not want any additional obstacles to contend with.

Unfortunately, that is exactly where we found ourselves. We were nearly a full boat's length—18.9 meters (62 feet)—behind Dartmouth. While this was unusual, it was not a complete surprise. It aligned with our race strategy to go out under control. We were concerned that something bad could happen in the chaos of the start. Two weeks earlier, when racing our chief rivals—Harvard and Princeton—one of our oarsmen had caught a crab within the first few strokes of the race. Catching a crab is when a rower loses control of his oar, and the blade gets trapped in the water by the momentum of the shell. The oar handle swings backwards, often going over the rower's head. We could not afford to have a repeat performance in today's race. Not today. And in some extreme cases, the rower may even be thrown overboard. If that happened, we would essentially be out of the race with no chance of winning.

Winning with Your Body, Mind, and Soul

Dartmouth's strategy was likely just the opposite. They knew we were a strong crew, especially late in the race. To beat us they would have to lay it all on the line. From start to finish. Build a lead that was insurmountable. Since we had raced Dartmouth earlier in the year, we knew they were fast off the line. Very fast. They had been our stiffest competition, and honestly, the only crew that had really pushed us during the regular season—which was good. They made us work harder after eking out a victory by four-tenths of a second in our initial race. Coming that close to losing and ruining a perfect season scared us. We wanted to go undefeated. We needed to go undefeated. Our unwavering desire—found long before the start of the race—was burned into our hearts and minds. It had propelled us to this pivotal moment.

Just a few years earlier, Yale had threatened to end the lightweight crew program. Thanks to the relentless letter-writing campaigns and heroic fundraising efforts of David Vogel, George Pew, and Dr. Stephen V. Flagg, the overall program was now out of the woods. However, there was still some talk—I didn't know if it was true or just a rumor—of ending the lightweight freshman rowing program.

The Yale lightweight freshmen crew team had not performed well in recent years. We needed to convince the university that ending the program would be a mistake. After all, it could be argued that collegiate rowing in the United States had started at Yale. And, subsequently, led to the birth of intercollegiate sports. "In 1843, the first American college rowing club was formed at Yale University. The Harvard–Yale Regatta is the oldest intercollegiate sporting event in the United States, having been contested every year since 1852 (excepting interruptions for wars and the COVID-19 pandemic)."[1]

Although we were behind after the start, it was no time to panic. I had a strong crew with an experienced stroke who knew how to win. Jamie Fosburgh, nicknamed Fos, was a seasoned oarsman and calm under pressure. He had a fierce competitive spirit. There was never any doubt about Fos's determination to win. Having rowed at Middlesex High School before Yale, he was used to rowing competitions and being a champion. "You have to be strategic about when to make your move in a race," he would say. And now was not the time to do it. We would settle into our race strategy and use the next eighteen hundred meters to close the gap—a little at a time. At least, that was the plan. However, it would not work out that way.

1. Wikipedia, "Rowing (sport)."

Chapter 1: The Start

Dartmouth had gotten faster. That narrow loss to us earlier in the year—their only defeat of the season—had also fueled them to get better. And they had. Over the next one thousand meters, there would be moves by us closing the gap then counter moves from Dartmouth reestablishing it. We tried several things: power tens for the boat, power tens for the engine, power tens by pairs, a burst of higher stroke rates, and deliberate lengthening of "run" to minimize drag on the boat. Nothing worked. And we were running out of water. Dartmouth was not fading as we had hoped. We *had* to take the stroke rate up—permanently.

As expected, Fos made his usual request for the current rate, and we agreed to take it up two. At thirty-six strokes per minute, we started to gain on Dartmouth after a few strokes. With five hundred meters to go, we had pulled even. My eyes now focused on the finish line. Poised to sprint pass them with a comfortable margin of victory. Then our worst nightmare came to life. One of our oarsmen caught a crab. Not one, but back-to-back crabs. Ouch! I thought Fos was going to come out of his seat and strangle the guy.

We lost all the momentum we had gained over the last five hundred meters. With three hundred meters to go, we were now half a boat's length down. I cannot say where the other crews were because I was 100 percent focused on Dartmouth. Not what I had been trained to do. But I knew we had to catch Dartmouth. It really didn't matter what the other crews were doing. If we did not catch Dartmouth, our pursuit of an undefeated season would be over.

Fos and I looked at each other. I could see the exhaustion in his face and in his body. Sweat dripped from strands of his dirty blond hair onto his vein-bulging neck, then made its way across his upper body before settling on his forearms momentarily. Its final act was rolling off his forearms to join the puddle sloshing back and forth under his number eight seat—the leader of the boat, the stroke. Of course, every seat in the boat is important, but none more so than his. From his seat, the standard is set. All other rowers, from number seven to number one—the bowman—strive to mimic the stroke's every move at precisely the same time. A near impossibility. But doable. And on those rare occasions when it happens, the crew experiences "swing." That old black magic.

The boat seems to move—or rather float on air, cloud nine, as if above the water—with just the slightest amount of effort. The only other sensation I have experienced that rivals it is runner's high. Merriam-Webster defines runner's high as "a feeling of euphoria that is experienced by some individuals engaged in strenuous running and that is held to be associated with a release of endorphins by the brain."[2] You do not ever fully understand how you achieved it. Yet you forever chase it, longing to make its acquaintance once again. And boy, did we need it now.

Having only two oarsmen with previous rowing experience, our boat had struggled earlier in the season. We had lots of raw talent. However, perfecting the rowing stroke, balancing the shell, and being perfectly synchronized with every other oarsman is not easy. It takes time, patience, and lots of practice—together, with the same group of guys. And it had all come together two weeks ago in the Harvard-Yale-Princeton race (H-Y-P). We had found our swing. Then we flew, or perhaps floated, down the course, winning with open water between us and our competitors. And in the process, we beat Princeton—who had not lost a race in nearly six years—on their home course and set a record that stood for many years. In the two weeks after the H-Y-P, leading up to the EARC Eastern Sprints, we even beat our varsity lightweight boat in practice on several occasions. So, we knew we could go fast. But could we find that swing, that speed, again—now, when we needed it most?

Fos was not sitting as tall at the catch—the start of the stroke—as he had been midway through the race. His shoulders were not as square during the stroke. And his back was not as straight at the finish—the end of the stroke. Despite the physical fatigue, I knew his mental state. He wanted to win. His body would recover, but he could not stomach losing—and certainly not the last race of the season, with everything on the line. Over the course of the season, we had developed nonverbal cues. Aside from Fos' occasional request for the stroke rating, words were not necessary. They just wasted energy. It was time to do whatever it would take to win. It was time to go all in.

---

2. *Merriam Webster.* "Runner's high."

Chapter 2: The Work

All life demands struggle. Those who have everything given to them become lazy, selfish, and insensitive to the real values of life. The very striving and hard work that we so constantly try to avoid is the major building block in the person we are today.

—Pope Paul VI

Plans are only good intentions unless they immediately degenerate into hard work.

—Peter Drucker

Knowledge comes, but wisdom lingers. It may not be difficult to store up in the mind a vast quantity of facts within a comparatively short time, but the ability to form judgments requires the severe discipline of hard work and the tempering heat of experience and maturity.

—Calvin Coolidge

"Come on, Hank. We're going to be late," Kendall yelled over his shoulder as he bolted out the door of our suite. I had not told anyone to call me Hank, rather it is the nickname given to most people named Henry. I did not introduce myself that way when meeting the five guys I would spend the next nine months with. Despite that, the name had caught on. And I was alright with it. So, I went with it. Freshman year at Yale University. A million miles from 476 Hazelwood Road. It still did not feel real.

LIMOUSINES

Forty-eight hours earlier, I was riding in a "limousine" from New York City. The service is called Connecticut Limousine, shortened to Connecticut Limo. However, the vehicles are not limousines—at least, not the one I was in. Just your typical van, oversized station wagon, or minibus. Now, the service does offer actual limousines or luxury cars, but I could not afford that.

It transports passengers from the major New York, New Jersey, and Connecticut airports to destinations throughout New England and beyond. The service shuttles bodies to and from John F. Kennedy International (JFK)—the busiest international air passenger gateway into North America and the busiest airport in the New York airport system[1]—LaGuardia (LGA), Newark Liberty International (EWR)—originally named Newark Metropolitan—and Bradley International (BDL). Owned and operated by the Connecticut Airport Authority, BDL is the second-largest airport in New England.[2] Considering the amount of business it does with Yale, Connecticut Limo had given the university its very own reservation portal. Every seat in my van was taken.

Students were arriving from all over the world. Yale is known for its international diversity, and the class of 1986 would be no exception. Sharing the limo with me were students from several states within the USA and several countries, including France and Italy. As it turned out, everyone was fluent in English. Now, of course, we didn't know that initially.

I have always been impressed by people who can speak multiple languages. I had studied French for four years—spanning my junior high and high school grades, seventh through tenth. With few opportunities to speak the language outside the classroom, I was never able to have a substantive conversation. And I certainly was not about to attempt one now. But to be polite, I did manage to say, "Bonjour. Je m'appelle Henri." The young man from France replied, "Je suis Philippe." Before he could continue, I very quickly interjected, "Parlez-vous anglais?" "Yes. Of course," said Philippe. He said it matter-of-fact like. As if stating the obvious.

I would learn over the next hour and forty-five minutes that Philippe had studied—and spoken—English for most of his life. It was very common for European citizens to speak multiple languages. I was informed that France, like many European countries, requires its citizens to have

---

1. Wikipedia, "John F. Kennedy International Airport."
2. Wikipedia, "Bradley International Airport."

Chapter 2: The Work

instruction in at least two foreign languages during their secondary education—the equivalent of junior high and high school in the USA. And while not mandatory, most students study English as their first foreign language. In fact, many students will have already had years of a foreign language, usually English, by the time they enter their secondary school. They would have been introduced to the language in kindergarten or pre-school (*l'école maternelles*) at age two or three and then continued their study of the language through their primary education (*l'école primaire* or *l'école élémentaire*) from age six to eleven. "So, don't buy it, Henri, if a European, especially a French person, says they don't speak English," Philippe advised me.

He was from Léon, a small town in the region of Landes in France. It is about seven hundred and thirty kilometers southwest of Paris on the Bay of Biscay and a stone's throw from the Spanish border. I had not heard of it. In fact, I was not familiar with hardly any French cities except Paris and Nice. But I was too embarrassed to admit that. Philippe, however, was quite familiar with many USA cities: New York, Chicago, Boston, Los Angeles, Dallas, and more. Apparently, USA geography is thoroughly covered at French primary and secondary schools.

We learned a great deal about each other during the ride. By the time we reached the entrance to Old Campus—so named since it is the oldest part of the Yale University campus—he knew I was from Memphis, Tennessee. The fifteenth of seventeen children—nine boys and eight girls. I had saved money for college by working at Chuck E. Cheese while in high school. My favorite color was blue. I pulled for the Minnesota Vikings whenever they played. Tennessee did not have a professional football team, so I threw my support to The Purple People Eaters. The stars held a special place in my heart. And as a child, I wanted to be an astronaut.

Philippe was the youngest of four—two boys and two girls. An average size family but quite small compared to mine. He and his family *loved* to travel and had visited several exotic places, including Hawaii, the Canary Islands, Fiji, and French Polynesia. I already knew he spoke English fluently and discovered he could also converse in Spanish, Italian, and a bit of German. His parents were both doctors, and his plan was to follow in their footsteps. But secretly, he wished he could someday compete in the French Grand Prix, formerly known as the Grand Prix de l'ACF (Automobile Club de France). He knew everything about the race, the cars, and the drivers. I learned that the French Grand Prix was one of the oldest motor races in the world as well as the first Grand Prix. Ferrari-built cars had won the race most often. And Juan Manuel Fangio, also known as El Maestro or El Chueco, had been crowned champion most often with five wins.

Chatting with Philippe made the drive seem shorter than it was. When the limousine stopped on College Street, its passengers spilled out onto the sidewalk with enthusiasm. Unfolding like accordions. Nostrils flaring and mouths opening, inhaling the clean, crisp autumn air. Arms reaching for the sky as heads rolled over hunched shoulders. Snap. Crackle. Pop.

To the west was Yale's distinctive Gothic architecture. To the east was the New Haven Green. The park buffers the university from some of the city's least desirable elements. During my four-year tenure at the school, I would discover that it did not always achieve its goal. In one incident, a female classmate was assaulted. And on one colorful, brisk fall afternoon, our room was broken into. Unfortunately for the burglar, he chose a room with several athletes—whose theme song could have been "Born to Run." He was overtaken in a foot race and held until the authorities arrived.

"It was nice meeting you. I hope someday you get to sit in the driver's seat of a Ferrari-built car at the French Grand Prix," I told Philippe. "Au revoir, Henri. I hope to see you around campus."

OLD CAMPUS

"Wait up. I'm coming!" I hollered back. Sliding on my sneakers—tennis shoes we called them in the South—I dodged the oversized chair placed too close to the door. Kendall was halfway down the stairs when the door slammed behind me. Within a few seconds, we emerged from the dorm's solid stone walls into an open courtyard. The stone walls were replaced by a wall of bodies. People everywhere you turned. It was chaotic. But organized chaos.

Our upper classmates and the organizations they represented had been waiting for this moment. It was their opportunity to recruit new members—fresh blood. Yale has over thirty men's and women's varsity teams and more than forty club sports. And that's not including intramural sports, which I learned were very popular and well organized within the Ivy League. Yale offered everything from archery to wushu. But only the major sports, football, basketball, baseball, etc., had the financial resources to conduct significant recruiting efforts before the start of the school year. The other sports, which were the majority, relied on the grassroots tactics

Chapter 2: The Work

on display in the courtyard. This was their first opportunity to persuade new talent to give their sport a try.

There were make-shift tennis courts, soccer fields, badminton courts, and lacrosse fields set up. Ping-pong balls and frisbees were flying everywhere. And then there were the crew boats, commonly referred to as shells. The word shell is used because the hull is only one-eighth to one-fourth inch thick to make the vessel as light as possible. All shells on display were made of composite materials such as carbon fiber, fiberglass, or Kevlar. Back at the boathouse, there were some vintage wooden boats, but they rarely left the boathouse. I had never seen a crew shell and had no knowledge of the sport. Did not even know crew was a sport.

The crew team had grabbed a prime spot—almost dead center—on Old Campus. It is where roughly two-thirds of all freshmen Elis reside for their inaugural academic year. They wanted a high-traffic area with the greatest panoramic view. Anyone with the slightest features resembling an oarsman, oarswoman, or a coxswain could be easily spotted. Every crew member's head was on a swivel.

My eyes were locked on Kendall's neon orange jacket, trying not to lose him in the crowd when I felt a tug on my arm. "Hey! You would make a perfect coxswain." "What did you just call me?" I asked, thinking to myself, "There's no way he just said what I think he said." Ignoring my question, the young man extended his hand in front of a set of sparkling white teeth. "Hi. I'm Kevin. You ever thought about rowing crew?" I wanted to say, "Hey, slow your roll dude. Where I come from, it's rude to grab people. I don't know you. And what the heck is crew?" Instead, I shook his hand. "Hi. I'm Henry, but I really don't have time to stop. I'm heading to an orientation briefing with my roommate." "Oh, you don't need to go to that right now. There will be more of those throughout the week. You can catch up with him later. Let me tell you about this amazing sport," he said with a big smile.

Over the next thirty minutes, I would learn that Kevin was the coxswain for the men's heavyweight junior varsity boat. The JV. More often referred to as the 2V. The big boys as he liked to say. He had been on the squad since arriving at Yale two years ago. He had always been on the heavyweight team and had worked his way up from the third varsity boat (3V), after coxing the first freshman boat (1F) in his inaugural year. Now going into his junior year as the 2V coxswain, he was pumped. There was no denying he loved the sport. He had taken to it like a fish to water when first introduced to it at his college-preparatory boarding school in Groton,

Massachusetts. And he was really excited about talking to me. We were almost identical in statue. Five feet, six inches tall and only a few pounds apart in weight. One hundred and fifteen pounds, give or take a few. We were also both African American, not that that mattered. I later discovered that Kevin had been the only African American on the Yale crew team for the previous two years.

The display put on by the crew teams—men's heavyweight, men's lightweight, and women—was impressive. The racing shells were sublime. Shining like new pennies under the bright autumn sun. The oars stretched out like giant feathers to form eagles's wings. Kevin told me a bit about the sport, including what the coxswain did. While the coxswain's main job is to steer the boat, the coxswain is also the on-the-water coach and strategist. He explained how the boat "worked." It was clear he had made the pitch before. He saved the best part for last. "And when you win, you get the losers' shirts—from *all* the boats in the race!" He showed me shirts from all the other Ivy League colleges—Brown University, Columbia University, Cornell University, Dartmouth College, Harvard University, Princeton University, and the University of Pennsylvania. Yeah, Yale had a good crew team.

CREW 101

A week later, I walked single file into Linsly-Chittenden Hall along with the rest of the crew team's new recruits. We paid no attention to the architectural marvel we were entering. Created by combining Chittenden Hall, a Romanesque Revival building erected in 1888–89, and Linsly Hall, built in 1906-7 as a Gothic building to join Chittenden and Dwight Halls, it is one of the most iconic structures on campus.

There were well over a hundred freshmen. Room/lecture hall 101 for the lightweight men, 110 for the heavyweight men, and the women down the hall in 120. I somehow ended up in room/lecture hall 101 with the lightweights. Not sure how that happened. After all, it was Kevin who convinced me to come to the meeting, and he was in room/lecture hall 110 with the heavyweights—the big boys. Nevertheless, I settled in. It was time to meet the coaches, trainers, and upperclassmen. Learn a lot more about the sport and ask any questions on our minds. Everything I heard sounded interesting, but there was one major problem. Crew was a water sport. And I didn't know how to swim.

Chapter 2: The Work

Yeah, you are sitting in a boat—shell—so you are not technically "in the water." "What if the boat flipped over or sank?" I asked. That is a near impossibility, I was assured. The shells are designed with decks at the sharp, pointed, canoe-type bow (fore) and the sharp, pointed, canoe-type stern (aft). These compartments measure roughly eight cubic feet and six and a half cubic feet at the bow and stern, respectively. Filled with air, they—along with the oars—provide sufficient buoyancy to keep the boat afloat. And that is the case even if it filled with water while all eight oarsmen and the coxswain are sitting in it. Then for an extra measure of safety, each oar can serve as a personal "life vest," able to float up to two hundred pounds. At one hundred and fifteen pounds soaking wet, I had nothing to worry about.

Of course, they neglected to mention the time-honored tradition of tossing the coxswain into the water after a victory. So, a few months later, when my crew grabbed my arms and legs after our first race and lifted me off the dock, I asked, "What the hell are you doing?" But no one was paying attention to the words coming out of my mouth. Probably didn't even hear me. It was pandemonium. Jumping. Yelling. High-fiving. Shirts—the losing team's jerseys—swirling over heads. The next thing I knew, I was in the water.

Then under the water. I had never been in water where my feet could not stand on a solid surface. I tried not to panic. Scenes from movies with people drowning flashed before my closed eyes. They always seemed to kick their legs and slap the water frantically with their arms. That only made the situation worse. So, I kept telling myself to relax. Just relax. And when I did, I floated back to the surface, then immediately screamed. "Guys. I can't swim!" No reaction from anyone. The celebration on the dock continued uninterrupted.

Down I went again. A few seconds later, my head popped above the surface. "Guys. I'm not kidding. I can't swim!" I think there was mild recognition that I might not be playing a joke. But still no movement towards me. Down I went again. When I came up for air the next time, I was determined to get someone's attention: "Hey, you _ _ _ _ _ _ _ idiots, I'm drowning here!"

And as I was heading under again, I saw a crewmate diving into the water. He grabbed ahold of my arm and pulled me to the dock. When we both finally got out of the water onto dry land, he asked our teammates, "Didn't you hear him say he can't swim?" They were still high on our victory and feeling good. So, somewhat laughing, they replied, "We thought he was joking. Who"—and probably thinking, but not saying, "in their right mind"—"would row crew without knowing how to swim?"

CREW 201

Tossing the coxswain in the water after a victory was not the only important fact left out during the question-and-answer session in Linsly-Chittenden Hall. Being in a part of the country with freezing temperatures during the fall, winter, and some of the spring, rowing on the water was not ideal for much of the year. As a result, the team had a relatively short racing season. A few head-style races in the fall then side-by-side intercollegiate competitions kicked off in the spring. The season—at least in the USA—concluded with the regional and national championship regattas in late spring as students were preparing for summer break.

But of course, that did not stop Yale from rowing on the water into late fall or even winter. It was a necessity to keep up with all the other Ivy League schools sprinkled throughout New England. In a sport where margins of victory are fractions of a second, no school could afford not to. The only exception was if the river was a block of ice. Pockets of frozen water were okay. The coaches would drive their motorized boats ahead of the crew shells to break up the ice so we could row through it.

Practicing outside in frigid weather is not uncommon for many outdoor sports. For most sports based on land, the only moisture to contend with is the athlete's own perspiration, and occasionally, rain, snow, or the morning dew. But for water sports, like crew, there are some *X* factors.

The wind always seems to blow harder on the water. Without the interference of hills, trees, and other man-made structures, it shoots across the surface unabated. Picking up speed, like a snowball rolling downhill. Slowing down momentarily as it slams into your body. Chilling you to the bone. Then there is the body of water you are on, or sometimes in. And even if the sport is meant to keep the athlete above water, some of it always seems to find its way onto your body. Like a magnet drawing metal shavings to it. An upside-down gravitational force. Now that is in addition to whatever moisture is falling onto you from above.

It becomes even more challenging when you need your fingers to perform a task. For rowers, the dexterity offered by the fingers to manipulate the oar's handle is a must. To adequately control the precise motions needed at the catch, throughout the stroke, and at the finish to feather the

Chapter 2: The Work

blade, the use of gloves is problematic. Of course, that didn't stop some guys from giving them a shot. However, they quickly discovered that they did not work. Once the gloves got wet, and they always did, it made matters worse. You might as well toss them overboard. A silver lining—if there was one—was the fact that the rowers' fingers were almost constantly in motion. So, it kept enough blood flowing to those extremities to prevent them from completely freezing. Coxswains were not so fortunate.

As Kevin had explained after grabbing me in the Old Campus courtyard, one of the coxswain's most critical duties is to steer the shell. The mechanism to steer the boat is a pair of wooden cylinders on each side of the coxswain's seat. A typical design would have them wrapped around a nylon cord/rope that is connected to the rudder. To control the rudder, and thus the boat, the cylinders are moved in the fore and aft directions. For example, to turn the boat to starboard, you would move the starboard cylinder forward (fore) toward the bow. Or alternatively, move the port cylinder backwards (aft) toward the stern. To turn the boat to port, you would move the port cylinder forward (fore) toward the bow. Or alternatively, move the starboard cylinder backwards (aft) toward the stern.

In an eight-man shell, having an equal amount of power on each side of the boat is a near impossibility. If the four guys rowing port generate more power than the four guys rowing starboard, then the boat will turn toward starboard. Conversely, it would turn toward port if the opposite were true. Depending on the power differential, without a correction, the boat could be considerably off course after a few strokes. And certainly, over the two thousand meters in a typical side-by-side race, you would be completely out of your lane. Interfering with the boat next to you, and most likely being disqualified. Therefore, the coxswain is constantly steering the boat—hopefully ever so slightly. When done well, it would be imperceptible to the oarsmen. Happening in the background without ever being detected.

All this to say that the coxswain's hands—fingers to be exact—are always wrapped around the cylinders. Very little movement, if any, of the fingers are required to manipulate the cylinders. So, no call for extra blood to flow to them during the ninety-minute practice session. When the shell pulled into the dock after a practice with freezing temperatures, it was not uncommon for the coxswain's hands to form a perfect C, frozen around the wooden blocks. Routine tasks—untying tennis shoes, buttoning or unbuttoning clothing, picking up a pencil or any small object, combing one's hair, etc.—would be impossible for at least half an hour. And that is after struggling to take a shower as hot as you could physically endure.

While the rowers did have the use of their fingers after coming off the water during freezing temperatures, there were other challenges that were just as daunting. Due to the natural friction generated from gripping the oar's handle while applying all the power you could muster, the palms of the hands took a beating. Literally. They were the first to absorb the jolt felt from thrusting the oar into the water while traveling at twelve-and-a-half miles per hour. They then had to withstand the pressure applied to pull the blade through the water during the stroke. And steady it as it exited the heavy water at the finish. Then finally they had to balance the blade with just the right amount of force and precision to feather it and carry it back to the catch. And in the process, create the least amount of drag as possible.

The repetition of these motions created blisters on every finger and throughout the palm. Sometimes covering the rower's entire palm. Now while the blisters were calloused, they would offer some protection against the hard, cold handle. Naturally, at some point the blisters would burst or peel. And when that happened . . . ouch! For some guys, this would go on throughout the entire season—alternating between tolerable and excruciatingly painful. But it was what the sport demanded. So, each rower found his way of dealing with it. Just as the coxswains found a way of overcoming mild frostbite at the end of practices with freezing temperatures.

CREW 301

"It's less than two weeks to weigh-in. You're five pounds overweight and some of the guys are nearly ten pounds overweight. What have you been eating?" I said to Fos. "You *have* to make weight." I know I didn't need to say it, but I said it anyway. He was the stroke of the first freshman boat, the standard. So, there was really no way around it. He had to set an example for the team. And, maybe even more important, for his boat. As the stroke, the other seven oarsmen take their lead from him, inside and outside the boat. When inside the boat, they seek to duplicate his every move, chasing perfect synchronization and that elusive swing. When outside the boat, they emulate his behavior as an extension of the team's discipline, code of conduct, and high standards.

To qualify as a freshman lightweight crew, the eight rowers had to average one hundred and fifty pounds. And no single rower could weigh

Chapter 2: The Work

more than one hundred and fifty-five pounds. Another important aspect of the coxswain's job was to monitor the guys' weights to ensure the boat would make weight come race day. My coach—a former coxswain himself—would say to the rowers, "You know your target race weight, and it's your responsibility to get there. No excuses." Then one-on-one with me, he would say, "It's your job to make sure the boat makes weight. If not, the boat will be disqualified from the race. And that will be on you." If you had four guys that were naturally heavier than one hundred and fifty-five pounds, chances are they were going to come in at one hundred and fifty-five pounds—or very close to it. That meant the other four guys had to average one hundred and forty-five pounds to meet the boat's overall requirement. We did not have many oarsmen in our boat whose normal weight was one hundred and forty-five pounds or less.

It was not unusual for my guys to be a few pounds overweight between races. But nearly ten pounds with under two weeks to go was a lot. A lot for any rower. And five pounds was a lot for Fos. However, he was not concerned. "I got this Hank. Don't worry. We'll make weight," he said confidently. Like it was no big deal. It is just business as usual. Something that is now a routine part of their brief college rowing careers.

Fos had a relatively straight-forward strategy to shed pounds: Eat as normally as possible to keep his strength up. A balanced diet of fruits and vegetables, meats and proteins, dairy, and grains. Drink nothing with calories. Only water, or coffee, or something like that. Count on dropping water weight over the last couple of days before the weigh-in.

For some of the other guys, their strategy was more intense: Reduce overall food intake. Eat half as many meals or eat half as much food at each meal. Reduce intake of foods not easily burned off. Those high in saturated fats—fast foods (burgers), whipped cream, fatty meats, fried foods, fatty snacks (corn chips), etc. Skip the salad dressing. And just say no to desserts. Expel any non-essential bodily fluids. Increase, intensify, and diversify workouts. Wear extra clothing during workouts to maximize sweating.

These activities would start immediately and continue until the weigh-in. A week before the weigh-in, if the excess pounds had not been cut in half, more actions would be taken. Meals would once again be cut in half. A rubber suit would be added to the workout wardrobe. At one or two days before the weigh-in, if the guy was not at race weight, he would go all in. No solid foods. Only water for liquids. Steam sauna two to four hours a day. In one previous desperate weight-making attempt, some guys sat in the sauna

Winning with Your Body, Mind, and Soul

with rubber suits on. It didn't work. In fact, it backfired. The suit prevents your body from sweating. And all this while continuing to train—row, lift weights, and run—for the upcoming race.

When the last rower stepped on the scales to weigh in for our final and biggest race of the year—the EARC championship—Fos and I breathed a sigh of relief. One hundred and fifty-five pounds, bringing the boat's average to one hundred and fifty pounds. Then almost immediately, I started to wonder how much the team had been affected—weakened—by this intense regiment over the past two weeks. When was the last time some of them had eaten a decent meal? How much power, both mental and physical, had they lost? The team needed to bring its *A* game. Not only the rowers, but everyone in the boat. Including me, the coxswain. We would not win without the entire boat firing on all cylinders.

For me, most of my work was mental. Studying the racecourse. Getting a forecast of the weather conditions at race time. Then developing several race strategies should the weather not agree with the forecast. Dissecting our opponents. Who was a fast starter? Who was the strongest finisher? Who had the year's best time on record for the race distance we were about to cover? Who had recently made changes in the lineup of their oarsmen? Any crew with a new stroke? And then on race day, having the mental clarity to turn the mountain of data into something useful. Information. Information to prepare and execute a winning race plan, while maintaining the ability to adjust if needed. To respond to a dynamic, fluid environment in real time. Overcome the known and, more importantly, unknown challenges that no amount of planning can foresee.

There was also some important physical work required. I had to have a strong voice, good reflexes to make steering adjustments as needed, and clear vision. Like the oarsmen, coxswains also had a weight requirement. Rather than a maximum weight—in order to qualify as a lightweight rower—the coxswain had a minimum weight. This was to prevent a boat from gaining an advantage by having to pull less "dead" weight. Since the coxswain is not actively engaged in rowing the boat, he/she is an extra load on the oarsmen. The minimum weight was set at one hundred and twenty-five pounds.

Any coxswain under the minimum weight had to carry sandbags to make up the difference. My normal weight was around one hundred and ten pounds, so I typically carried roughly fifteen pounds of sand with me into the boat. Or at least that is what the math would suggest. However,

Chapter 2: The Work

that is not what I did. To minimize the amount of "dead" weight, I would drink as much water as possible before the weigh-in. I once consumed a gallon—nearly eight-and-a-half pounds—of water in the span of about thirty minutes. Then after the weigh-in, I would use various methods to get rid of the water. The most natural—and probably effective—method was the body's normal way of emptying the bladder—urinating. But if that didn't work—or work fast enough—more unconventional methods would be called upon. You can use your imagination. Probably not pretty. But if it could give us an advantage, then I was all in.

Chapter 3: The Finish

The last thing you want to do is finish playing or doing anything and wish you would have worked harder.

—Derek Jeter

Much of the stress that people feel doesn't come from having too much to do. It comes from not finishing what they've started.

—David Allen

Starting strong is good. Finishing strong is epic.

—Robin Sharma

It was time to put the work to work. We had to go faster. Dartmouth was not slowing down, as we had hoped. In crew, the boat goes faster with either the oarsmen pulling harder or by taking more strokes in the same amount of time—and in the ideal world, accompanied by swing. And if you really wanted to—or needed to in our case at that moment—go faster, you did both. So, what did we do? I yelled, "Up two in two!"

That is the command to add two strokes per minute to the current rate after completing the next two strokes. We were rowing at a comfortable thirty-six strokes per minute; about the same rate we had rowed a few weeks earlier at the H-Y-P. So, this took the rate to thirty-eight strokes per minute. After four or five strokes, I issued the same command, "Up two in two!" At forty strokes per minute, lots of things can go wrong. The risk of someone catching a crab increases greatly. If that happened, our chances at a victory would almost certainly disappear. Even if something worse happened to Dartmouth, we would both be overtaken by another crew in the race.

Chapter 3: The Finish

With one of my oarsmen already catching back-to-back crabs at a lower stroke rate, that was certainly on my mind. But now was not the time to worry about that. With just over one hundred meters to go and still three seats down, we had to risk it all. I screamed, "Up two in two. We are not going to lose this race!" Fos responded, jacking the rate to a dangerous forty-two strokes per minute. And the boys in the boat followed. We started to move. Two seats down with eighty meters to go. "Keep your eyes in the boat. Press your knees down. Don't rush the catch. Don't hang at the catch. Up tall at the finish." At this first-time-ever racing stroke rate, these fundamentals would make us winners or losers.

Fifty meters to go—about three strokes—and still one seat down. Every stroke had to be executed flawlessly, with precision and power. Now was the time to trust our conditioning, both physical and mental. The hundreds of hours spent preparing our bodies for the physical challenge. The thousands of pounds lifted in increments commensurate with each person's strength. Repetition after repetition. Pulling against the unrelenting ergometer. Running the never-ending stairs, eleven flights from the basement to the roof, of Payne Whitney Gymnasium—the second-largest gym in the world by cubic feet and commonly referred to as the cathedral of sweat.[1] The early morning rows with barely enough sunlight to see the shoreline. Then the late evening rows—on the water and in the tanks—requiring a flat-out sprint to the dining hall to keep from going to bed on an empty stomach. Taking advantage of every waking moment outside the classroom. Pushing the body beyond its limits—some just set within the last twenty-four hours. Constantly raising the bar. Building muscle and muscle memory to execute the perfect stroke.

Equally important as our bodies, our minds had to be worked. The countless hours spent preparing our minds for the mental challenge. Cultivating an ability to block out all distractions. To have a singular, tunnel-vision focus that puts you in an altered state. A trance. The only thing you are aware of is the task at hand. The race. The feel of the boat. The device in your hands. The voice in your head. The movements of your body. Each person had his own way of getting into the zone, or as three Yale researchers would say, getting into the flow:

> The basic equation underlying their [Ryan Carlson, currently a principal researcher with the University of Chicago Booth School of Business, David Melnikoff, an assistant professor of organizational

---

1. Wikipedia, "Payne Whitney Gymnasium."

behavior at the Stanford Graduate School of Business, and Paul Stillman from the Ohio State University's Department of Psychology] computational theory of flow is relatively simple: it computes the mutual information between desired end states and means of attaining them, a quantity expressed as I(M;E). . . . "Our theory says that the more informative a means is, the more flow someone will experience while performing it," Melnikoff said.[2]

Without the assistance of the mathematical formula proposed by the Yale researchers, each rower had found what works for him. A personal formula created from years of trial and error. On-the-job training. Sharpened over his lifetime. Most began with getting the proper amount of sleep the night before and various behaviors typically associated with meditation or mindfulness. Whatever technique worked best for each person.

And if fate—along with a heaping dose of desire and ability—was on our side, we would prevail.

I was not in a rower's seat, but I knew the physical and mental state of my oarsmen. As a distance runner, I had felt the white-hot burn of my thighs when sprinting to the finish line of a cross-country race. The lack of oxygen in my lungs. Making each breath seem like it was my last. I imagined their backs and shoulders aching after pulling against the heavy water for nearly two thousand meters (1.24 miles). Muscling the oar through the lake's chilly waters with their arms, wrists, and hands. Some of those hands blistered and bleeding. Propelling the boat forward by driving their legs down from their upside-down *V* position. Every muscle in their bodies screaming for more blood flow. More oxygen. While it's not a weight-bearing sport, according to Wikipedia, "rowing is one of the few sports that exercises all the major muscle groups including quads, biceps, triceps, lats, glutes, and abdominal muscles."[3]

Did they have doubts about their own abilities? Do I have what it takes to be a champion? And if they did not doubt their own personal ability, what about the guy behind them or in front of them? Could we summon the courage, drive, and determination as a team to catch Dartmouth a second time? Had each person formed a mental picture of themselves—like many world-class athletes who frequently rely on visualization to help them win major sports competitions—crossing the finish line first? The body cannot achieve what the mind cannot conceive. And if there were no doubts

2. Hathaway, "Getting in the Flow."
3. Wikipedia, "Rowing (sport)."

Chapter 3: The Finish

about those things, then was there enough distance left in the race to catch them? After all, oarsmen cannot see what is up ahead. They face opposite the direction in which the boat is traveling.

Two strokes left. A half a seat down. My eyes darting back and forth between my crew and Dartmouth. They still looked strong, but we were clearly gaining on them—again. And my hope was that their oarsmen knew this. When you know another boat is catching you, it affects you. Both mentally and physically. You lose focus. Instead of concentrating on the guy in front of you and what is happening in your boat, you get distracted by what is happening in the competitor's boat. Something completely out of your control. Compounding the mental distraction, your body parts also get suckered into the act. Your eyes start wandering. This is a recipe for disaster. And to overcome it, we must fight vehemently against our human nature. Any oarsmen will tell you that one of a coxswain's most common phrases is, "Eyes in the boat." Bad things happen when oarsmen do not follow this direction.

Was that a chink in Dartmouth's armor? Was that splash of water at the boat's bow larger than the normal splash? Did the number four seat get his oar stuck at the finish—a crab—even if only a small one? Or was this just wishful thinking on my part? I was desperate for any sign that we could make up three feet with one stroke remaining. Or had we already crossed the finish line? Sitting at the stern of the boat—about fifty feet from the bow ball—the coxswain can't tell the exact moment the finish line is breached. But, based on my experience and visual clues, I knew it was close. Very close.

I crossed the finish line exactly parallel with the Dartmouth coxswain. We both understood that the race had already been decided—a little over two seconds earlier—when our boats' bows had crossed the line. "Weigh enough," I commanded. Probably as a whisper. My voice completely shot from yelling at the top of my lungs for the past few minutes. All oars emerged from beneath the surface, then crashed back down onto the water with a heavy splat. One by one the oarsmen collapsed onto the handles. Across their laps or tucked under their arms. Whatever position felt most natural for each person. That is, all except Fos. He was still in the zone. Fatigue would not hit him until back on dry land. He looked at me with the question written on his face. "Who won?" I didn't know. There was no signal from the official at the finish line.

Winning with Your Body, Mind, and Soul

In crew, it is tradition for the losing team to award the winners with their jersey—an activity referred to as shirt-racing or shirt-betting. It is unclear exactly when, where, or how the tradition began.

"Presumably, shirt-racing is so old that no one remembers how it began, only romanticizing further the practice. But [Thomas] Weil suggests that the betting of shirts may have been introduced by a Syracuse crew in 1920, or even more recently than that. While Weil's collection includes stories of shirt-racing dating back to the '20s and '30s, the collector has never seen an image of the practice before the '60s. Weil further emphasized that one can be sure of shirt-racing's 20th-century origins since, pre-1900, racing was done primarily without shirts."[4] We do know that the gesture of giving someone the shirt off your back did not originate with crew. That distinction belongs to Tobias Smollett, who coined it in his 1771 novel *Humphry Clinker*.[5] But whatever its origins were, it was now deeply entrenched in the sport.

Depending on weather conditions, the exchange would take place back on the dock after the crews had disembarked from the boat. But to follow true tradition or for significant races—and this was certainly one of those—the losing boat would row over to the winners and give them their racing jerseys right there on the water. It was a sign of respect, honor, and admiration for the victors in an epic battle. But I did not know the outcome of the race. And looking at the Dartmouth coxswain, it was clear he did not know either. So, both boats remained in their lanes—waiting.

As the seconds, then minutes—which seemed like hours—ticked by, the oarsmen began to regain their strength. Drenched with their own perspiration and the cool lake water, the air was now sending a slight chill through their battered bodies. There was still no word from the race officials. Whoever ended up being the victor would have to collect their opponents' shirts on dry land.

We rowed to the dock and proceeded with the familiar routine of exiting the boat. Slowing the shell gradually as it approached the dock. Working as a couple from the bow forward. Dropping pairs of rowers until the stroke and number seven brought us back to dry land. Then following a similar routine to exit the shell—by pairs, to keep the boat stable in the water, with the coxswain being the last to disembark.

---

4. Borek, "Oarsmen Must Win."
5. The Free Dictionary, "Give the Shirt."

Chapter 3: The Finish

My mind drifted back to our race with Dartmouth about a month ago. Without any stiff competition before that race, we were not fully prepared for such a fierce battle. We probably had not trained as hard as we could—should—have. But thankfully, we still came out victorious. To ensure we didn't make that mistake in this race, we had trained extremely hard. On the water rowing at least twice a day, including weekends. Longer runs. More weight training—for both strength and endurance. Had we over trained? Peaked too soon? Was the intense weight loss routine by Fos and some of the other rowers all for naught? Had the five pounds of water weight I shed between the weigh-in and the starter's pistol made a difference?

It had now been upwards of fifteen minutes since the race ended. Everyone was standing on pins and needles. And then the announcement. "Ladies and gentlemen, thank you for your patience. By photo finish, here are the official results of the 1983 EARC Eastern Sprints Grand Finals for the Men's Lightweight Freshman. Finishing sixth with a time of 6:59.9, Navy. In fifth place, with a time of 6:54.8, Princeton. In fourth place, with a time of 6:48.2, Cornell. In third place, with a time of 6:47.7, Harvard. In second place, with a time of 6:44 even, Dartmouth. And the winner, with a time of 6:43.8 [about three feet ahead of Dartmouth], and a *new course record*, Yale!"

The feeling that went through my body—and I am sure through each of my teammates—is indescribable. The aches and pains disappeared instantly. The color in Fos's face returned after appearing ashen white when he had gotten out of the boat a few minutes ago—the full measure of fatigue having hit him like a tsunami making him dizzy and off balanced. My voice returned like it had never been lost. It was replaced by a light-headed euphoria high above the noise around me. My eyes filled with water until my lids could not contain it. Tears flowed freely. Affirmation that all the hard work had paid off. The whole crew embraced. A big gnarly bear hug. Pure joy.

Reflections

When did life start for you?

_____
_____
_____
_____
_____

What is the most important work you are doing
for your physical well-being?

_____
_____
_____
_____
_____

What have you left unfinished?

_____
_____
_____
_____
_____

PART II: WINNING WITH YOUR MIND

Do not conform to the pattern of this world, but be transformed by the renewing of your mind. Then you will be able to test and approve what God's will is—his good, pleasing and perfect will.

—Romans 12:2 (NIV)

Chapter 4: Mind Over Matter

> External circumstances can only cause you physical pain.
> Suffering is created in your mind.
>
> —Sadhguru

> The mind is like water. When it's turbulent, it's difficult to see.
> When it's calm, everything becomes clear.
>
> —Prasad Mahes

> You have power over your mind, not outside events.
> Realize this, and you will find strength.
>
> —Marcus Aurelius

It was a sound I would never forget—could never forget. It was the closest man-made sound to the crackling of a lightning bolt splitting apart a massive oak tree. Once you have heard it, you cannot unhear it. The sound was being repeated—and increasing in frequency. It was accompanied by what felt like electrical shocks in random places throughout my twelve-year-old body. I was in excruciating pain. But I was determined not to cry.

My father was beating me with a genuine rawhide belt—now blackish brown in color with the mixture of red blood on it. My blood. I called it Killer. To inflict maximum damage, he would soak Killer in water. "Take off your shirt," he had ordered. That was twenty minutes ago. I felt each lash as the wet monster dug into my skin. But my mind was somewhere else. It was almost as if I was watching the whole ordeal from a distance, like my mind and body were disconnected—two separate organisms having two separate experiences. Or perhaps it was one organism having two different reactions to the same experience.

Idealists would argue that this is completely understandable since the external physical world is not real. They maintain that the mind is all that exists. Idealists believe that the external physical world is either mental itself or an illusion created by the mind. Dualists would also contend that this is understandable since the mind and body are two separate and distinct things. Therefore, it is reasonable to conclude that each "thing" can have a different experience or reaction to the same situation, set of circumstances, or stimuli. Which perspective is correct remains to be seen. In either case, it was a technique—or even perhaps an ability/skill—I had been perfecting for some time. Of course, it was nothing on the level of what Jack Schwarz was able to do. Nonetheless, it was significant for me.

> Jack Schwarz was a Dutch Jewish writer who was captured by the Nazis and sent to a concentration camp like millions of others. He was beaten and tortured beyond comprehension. And it was at that point that something unusual happened according to Schwarz. He realized he could control and regulate the pain he endured. He undertook a practice of meditation and prayer. He sharpened his mind to the point where he could withstand torture and horror.
>
> At the end of WWII, Schwarz started speaking out about the power of love and prayer with a higher self. To demonstrate he would go around Europe and demonstrate on himself. Schwarz would press lit cigarettes into his flesh and no burn marks would show up. He would [stick] knives and needles through his organs and the holes would close up without bleeding or pain. He would press himself on to a bed of nails and speak on the power of prayer.
>
> Schwarz wasn't trying to say he was exceptional. In fact he was making a point that his mind was the same as everyone else and it is there from which he was able to tap into that power. The power he was tap[p]ing into was, according to him, God.[1]

Like Schwarz, my ability was developed out of sheer necessity. Living under the same eight hundred square-foot roof with twelve other people for most of my childhood, there was no such thing as alone time. No safe space. Rarely a quiet moment. Something was *always* going on. And it didn't stop just because I had homework. Or anything else that required a serene, noiseless environment. I learned to block out all external activity with a single-minded focus on the task at hand. Totally dialed in. As a child, I, of course, was not aware of any peripheral or long-term benefits from this practice.

1. Aurin, "Six Perfections."

Chapter 4: Mind Over Matter

> Spending even 15 minutes on mental health hygiene each day can bring a host of benefits, from improved mood and better relationships to . . . deeper concentration and enhanced creativity. . . .
>
> For some people, mental health hygiene means dedicating a few minutes of their morning routine to meditation, stretching or walking—but [Stanford professor of psychiatry and behavioral sciences Hui Qi] Tong [who has served as the director of the Mindfulness Program at the Stanford Center for Integrative Medicine since 2019] says just about any activity can qualify, as long as you are paying attention to what you are doing while you perform the task. . . .
>
> She [Tong] encourages anyone interested in the concept of mental health hygiene to find what works for them by experimenting with bringing mindful attention to different activities.[2]

My mindful behavior sometimes annoyed my mom, Dee La, who would have to call my name several times before I responded. And if she was really upset, calling several of my brothers' names before finally yelling, "You know who I'm talking to. Get your behind in here!" Or, my siblings, who would have to pinch me to "bring me back" to this world. But it was what I needed to do. Had to do, if I wanted to achieve my desire of going to college. Make it out of the conditions into which I was born. My family did not have the financial resources to send me or any of my siblings to college. And since I was not gifted with a physique or skill set to earn an athletic scholarship, it would have to be through academics. "Use your head for more than a hat rack," Dee La would say. So, I did. Going all in.

My father was becoming more frustrated and irritated with each stroke. Because I would not cry or admit to something I had not done. I was not a crybaby. However, I did shed tears rather easily. But this time was different. My father—and my siblings—knew that I was known for telling the truth. Even if it meant I was going to get a lashing. So, when I said, "Dad, I didn't do it." I expected him to believe me. Besides, I could not have done it. I was not even in the room when it occurred. Exactly what "it" was, I do not remember. But since my two younger brothers, Marvin and Allen, would not confess, all of us boys were going to get a beating. Starting with me, the eldest of the three remaining boys in the house. My older sister, Deborah, was also present. Yet mysteriously she was not at risk. Apparently, "it" could only have been done by a boy.

---

2. Leggett, "Mental Health Hygiene."

Killer was not doing its job. So, my father abandoned it and resorted to his fists. He was now punching me like I was a grown man. Striking me with enough force to send me crashing to the floor with each blow. "Get up," he demanded. Another blow. And the routine repeated for the next five minutes. Water was now escaping my eyes. Flowing over my cheeks. But I was not crying, and I think that shook my father. He came to realize—what I had already decided at the start of the ordeal—that I was not going to cry. And I was not going to confess to something I did not do. What he and I didn't know was the decision I would make afterwards. When he finished with me, he moved on to Marvin.

I stepped out of the line of fire and stood next to Deborah. She later told me that my lips had turned a blueish-purple color. Evidently that is what happens to your body parts when they are deprived of blood or oxygen. I said, "If he ever lays his hands on me again, that will be his last time." I do not think my father could hear my words, or if the words even escaped my lips. But he didn't need to hear me. My clenched jaws and piercing eyes were screaming loud enough.

My mind had already moved on to planning his death, because I did not expect him to change his disciplinary tactics. They usually started with something one of us boys had done that did not meet with his approval. We never knew exactly what was allowed and what was forbidden. In many cases, the rules were not spelled out. Some things, of course, were crystal clear. No talking back to him. No running in the house. No cussing. No fighting one another. No sitting in *his* chair. And never, never, never turn on the television without his permission. Everything else depended on his mood. A certain action one day would bring a smile and praise. On a different day, we could be beaten to within an inch of our life for the same action. We were in constant suspense and fearful of doing or saying the wrong thing—at the wrong time.

While I was certainly afraid of my father's wrath, I was more afraid of Jesus' wrath. Being reared—at least by my mother—as a Christian, I was taught not to lie. "God don't like a liar," Dee La would say. "You can only get to heaven by telling the truth, even if it hurts." By this point in my life, John 8:32—"And you shall know the truth, and the truth shall make you free" (NKJV)—was already firmly imprinted on my mind. So, I told the truth. Even if it meant a beating for me and any sibling—to their disappointment—who was also a culprit of the misconduct. This was common

Chapter 4: Mind Over Matter

knowledge within the family. Now, I was not a tattletale. But if asked, I was not going to lie.

And if no one confessed, then everyone got beat. Starting with the eldest of the group at the time, me, and working down to the youngest, Allen. On these occasions, I wanted to be Allen. The last one to go under Killer. By that time, much of dad's strength—and often his fury—had left him. Used up on me and Marvin. I of course took the brunt of it, being first in line. And that is what made me so angry with this latest beating. Everyone knew I had not done "it." But the truth did not matter.

As fate would have it, I never had to act on my plan. Shortly after that day, my father called Dee La, who had moved away a year ago. "Sis"—that was his nickname for her—"you have to come get two of the kids. I cannot handle all four of them." I do not know what brought him to that conclusion, but I suspect my act of defiance had something to do with it. I believe it was a pattern my father had noticed in his children as they became a certain age. The age varied by child.

For one of my brothers, the age was ten, when he shot my father with his own .38-caliber revolver. My brother's solution to end the senseless abuse inflicted on him. And more specifically, as retaliation for a brutal, black-eyed, sunglasses-covering beating mom had suffered.

For one of my brothers, the age was fifteen, when he stepped in to engage in a fist fight with my father. He did so with the knowledge it would probably lead to his eviction from the house—another brother had been kicked out for simply refusing to cut his hair. Despite the risk to his body or his living arrangements, he had to protect Dee La from the punches being thrown by my father. And as he suspected, the next morning he was homeless.

For one of my sisters, the age was twenty-one. After learning of mom's cracked ribs from a recent "accident," she returned to the house clutching a .357 Smith & Wesson Magnum. She stepped into the house and swore to blow my father's mother _ _ _ _ _ _ head off if he rose from *his* chair as she extracted Dee La from her nightmare at 476 Hazelwood Road.

For me, the age was twelve, after enduring the last beating, even with the truth on my side, I would ever take from my father. I had had enough—more than enough.

We were asked who wanted to stay with our father and who wanted to go with our mother. "Can't we *all* go with mom?" Even as I asked the question, I already knew the answer. No. It was clear Marvin and Allen, the two youngest, should stay together. Which meant Deborah and I would stay together. So, the only question remaining was which pair would go with mom and which pair would stay with dad. I'm not completely sure how the decision was made, but Marvin and Allen packed their things, and we said our goodbyes.

Chapter 5: Mind Games

We must have strong minds, ready to accept facts as they are.

—Harry S. Truman

The test of a first-rate intelligence is the ability to hold two opposed ideas in mind at the same time and still retain the ability to function.

—F. Scott Fitzgerald

Whatever you hold in your mind will tend to occur in your life. If you continue to believe as you have always believed, you will continue to act as you have always acted. If you continue to act as you have always acted, you will continue to get what you have always gotten. If you want different results in your life or your work, all you have to do is change your mind.

—Anonymous

FIVE WINTERS HAD COME and gone since Deborah and I said goodbye to Marvin and Allen. The first two years in separate households and the last three under the same roof. With our mother. As it turned out, our father could not handle any of the kids.

I was now in my senior year of high school with Marvin a year behind me and Allen two years behind Marvin. It had been six weeks since I submitted my final college application. Packages had gone to five colleges including Harvard, Yale, and Princeton. Members within a group of schools—the Ivy League (also known as the Ancient Eight)—I was vaguely aware of when I began high school. Grades ten through twelve. I had heard their names but knew nothing about them except that they were old and very expensive. And applying to them was not my idea. At least not initially.

Winning with Your Body, Mind, and Soul

Entering Northside High School in the fall of 1979, I was carrying the highest grade-point average (GPA) for the class. I, of course, did not know that walking into the school on day one. It was revealed to me by my guidance counselors Ms. Martha "Marty" Watkins and Dr. Glenda Cryer in one of our early sessions. Even before gaining that knowledge, I had already set my sights on graduating a few years later at the top of my class—valedictorian.

With sixteen siblings—fourteen of them older than me—I had plenty of competition to fuel my scholastic aspirations. The Davis family had never had anyone finish their schooling as valedictorian. An older sister, Terry, had come the closest. She had graduated from high school a few years earlier at the number two spot—salutatorian. She was also the first of my siblings to graduate from college. Receiving a bachelor of science degree in electrical engineering from Kansas State University. The same degree I would earn five years later from a different university.

Higher education was not intentionally encouraged within my family. You were not explicitly discouraged from pursuing it, but it depended on which parent you paid more attention to. Neither of my parents finished high school. My father completed only the third grade, and my mother stopped her education after the eleventh grade. My mother always expressed a desire to finish her high school education and get her degree—her diploma. My father, on the other hand, had no regrets or desires for more schooling. He did not see the need for it or the value in it. He often boasted about only having a third-grade education and doing fine in life. So, you can probably guess his perspective on higher education. Nonetheless, we were rewarded for good grades, at least during elementary school. Twenty-five cents for every *A*, ten cents for every *B*, and a nickel for every *C*. I liked getting *A*'s.

Among other things, the guidance counselor's role was to help students figure out what they wanted to do after high school. I knew I wanted to go to college but had not given much thought to where that might be. My first year of high school was nearing the end when I had a meeting with Ms. Watkins and Dr. Cryer. It was our normal routine to meet about once a month. They wanted to know if I had any specific plans for the summer. I did not. Starting at twelve years of age, I had always worked during the summer. A necessity to help with home finances. Jobs such as cutting grass, washing cars, selling newspapers, and selling candy were the most common. I had no reason to think this summer would be any different. My counselors had other plans.

Chapter 5: Mind Games

"We would like you to apply to summer school," they said. I thought to myself, "I must not have heard them correctly. Did they say *apply* to summer school? Why in the world would I want to do that?" Summer school is for students who screw up during the regular school year and need the summer to make up for their folly. I am at the top of the class. And besides, my family depends on the money I earn during the summer for its livelihood. I said, "What exactly do you mean?" "Let us explain," they went on.

"There are several private high schools—boarding schools actually—in New England that offer a certain number of scholarships to attend their summer program. The summer program helps prepare students for college. We think this would be an excellent program for you to attend." Probably by the look on my face, they could tell I was not sold. "You don't have to decide now," they assured me. "Here is some information on the schools and their programs. Take it home. Read it over and discuss it with your family. We will talk again in a few days." Trying to keep an open mind, I took the pamphlets and agreed to look them over.

When I got home, I discovered the counselors had had the same conversation with my sister Deborah. Deborah was one year older and one grade higher than me. She was also near the top of her class—sitting at the number four spot for the highest GPA. After talking with each other and our mother, we decided to apply. We could not pass on the potential opportunity at this point. Our logic was if we get accepted, we can always say no should circumstances change. There were enough siblings at home to help with the family finances during the summer, so our contribution would not be missed too much. A few days later, Deborah and I met with the counselors and obtained the applications. We returned them the following week and began the waiting period.

It's ironic how your attitude changes after you have applied for something. Even if you were not initially interested in the thing, once you apply, you want to be accepted. Or in a more general sense, once you make a commitment to anything you want to achieve it. To succeed. To be a winner. Maybe it is part of our innate need for self-esteem identified in Maslow's hierarchy at level four. Whatever the reason, I was anxious for a response. And hopefully a positive one.

The response came a few weeks later. I was accepted to Phillips Academy (also known as Phillips Academy Andover, Andover, or simply PA) in Andover, Massachusetts. My sister Deborah was not. She did, however, receive a certificate of merit as a prep school candidate. It had not occurred to us that one of us might be accepted and not the other. We had not discussed that possibility and were not prepared to deal with the real situation we now faced.

Should I decline the scholarship? Can I offer my spot to Deborah? After all, I can reapply next year in my junior year. However, there was no way of knowing if I would be accepted. The schools were highly selective, admitting roughly 15 percent of applicants. But I was willing to take that chance if it meant my sister could take my spot. She is in her junior year, so this is her one and only opportunity. I didn't know how these things worked. I did not know what to do. So, I turned to my counselors for guidance.

They explained, to my disappointment, that I could not transfer my scholarship to Deborah. I certainly could decline the scholarship. Unfortunately, there was no way of assuring it would be awarded to Deborah. It would be awarded to another student, but I had no control over that. A few months later, I was on a bus from Memphis heading to Andover.

It was at Phillips Academy where I was officially introduced to the Ivy League. I would discover that Phillips Academy was the oldest incorporated academy in the United States. And that "Andover traditionally educated its students for Yale, just as Phillips Exeter Academy educated its students for Harvard, and Lawrenceville prepped students for Princeton."[1] Many, in fact, the majority of students at the academy had their sights set on Yale. And if not Yale, one of the other seven colleges that make up the Ivy League. Some were blazing new trails to be the first in their family to attend one of these colleges. Others would be following in the footsteps of a long line of relatives before them with an Ivy League degree. Taking their place as an integral member of their family's legacy.

After the summer, I returned to Northside for my junior year. For me, the landscape of potential colleges had forever changed. My perspective broadened exponentially. I completed the school year sitting at the top of the class with the highest GPA. For the summer, I reverted to my previous routine of working to help support the family. Upon my return to Northside for my senior year, my guidance counselors eagerly informed me that they had acquired college applications from Harvard, Yale, and Princeton. I was not surprised. "You can apply to any other schools you'd like to," they explained. "But you have to apply to these three schools."

Northside High School was not known for its academic prowess. No student in the school's thirteen-year existence had ever been accepted to an Ivy League college. Much less graduated from one. But my counselors'

---

1. Wikipedia, "Phillips Academy."

Chapter 5: Mind Games

hope was not dimmed. I too was optimistic. I had crammed as many advanced placement (AP) classes into my schedule as possible. As a result, I had maintained the highest GPA—4.3 on a 4.0 scale—in my class throughout my high school years. I had also held leadership positions in several extracurricular activities. President of the student body and president of the school's chapter of the National Honor Society. Holding both positions while working at least twenty hours a week at Chuck E. Cheese. My classmates had also bestowed upon me the title of "Most Likely to Succeed." And about the same time college applications were due, I was selected as the first alternate to "Teenager of the Year" by the Memphis Press-Scimitar. Even with these accolades under my belt, getting accepted into an Ivy League school would be difficult. If successful, I would be the first in my family and the first from my high school.

The applications were submitted, and once again, the waiting game.

When a letter from the Yale Office of Admissions arrived a few weeks later, I was excited. But at the same time, I was reluctant to open it. What if I had been rejected? Although I had not set my sights on an Ivy League school in the beginning, I now wanted to be accepted—since I had applied. "Ok. Just get on with it," I said to myself.

The letter did not begin like a typical acceptance or rejection letter. It explained that applicants are required to undergo an interview as part of the evaluation process. If a prospective student could not come to New Haven, Connecticut, the interview could take place in their local geographical area. It would be conducted by a Yale alum. My interview had been scheduled for the following week in Germantown, Tennessee.

Germantown is a city next to Memphis. A suburb in fact, bordering it on the east-southeast. It is where the rich people live. I had never been to Germantown and did not know anyone who lived there. Driving to the address, I was thankful for allowing myself extra time to get to the house. The directions were good, so it was not difficult to find the home. The extra time was needed to admire the houses along the way. Houses unlike any I had ever seen, except on television or in a magazine. The garages were bigger than my entire house. And some structures were hundreds of yards from the street. At the end of driveways that could have served as public roads in my neighborhood. By the time I arrived at my destination, my mind was made up. I had decided this is where I wanted to live. And if going to Yale could make that a reality, then I wanted to go to Yale.

My newly formed decision was reinforced when I pulled into the driveway of my interviewer's home. It was a massive brick structure with a garage—yes, the size of my house. I parked in the driveway. A set of designer stairs made a gradual ascension to a porch that stretched the length of the house's front face. Rocking chairs had been positioned in strategic locations to enjoy early morning sunrises or late afternoon sunsets. Spaced perfectly under a row of overhead fans—outdoors! I rang the doorbell.

When the gentleman opened the beautifully carved wooden door, I was blinded by a dazzling chandelier. "Hello. You must be Henry. Please come in." Extending his hand, he introduced himself. "I'm Brian." While in complete awe of my surroundings, I shook his hand and did manage to say, "Hi. I'm Henry. You have a lovely home."

After making small talk in the foyer, Brian led me to his office. With three of the four walls covered—floor to ceiling—with books, it could have just as easily been a library. The chair behind the desk faced the door. He motioned for me to sit in a chair on the opposite side of the mahogany masterpiece. With my back to the door, which made me a bit uneasy. I have never been comfortable not being able to see what's coming at me. He proceeded by explaining the Yale admissions process and his role within that process. Much of this I already knew from the letter I had received from Yale a week or so ago. But it was good to hear it again. It also helped me to relax. I am the type of person—and I do not think I am alone—that feels more comfortable with more information. It alleviates my human nature to fear the unknown.

After going on for what seemed like an eternity, Brian finished with the process overview. He lowered his wire-rimmed reading glasses, looked straight at me, and said, "So, Henry. I have your resume here, but tell me about yourself." At this point in my life, I had been interviewed enough times to respond to this request in my sleep.

For the next fifteen minutes, I introduced him to Henry Arnold Davis. The public version. The soon-to-be valedictorian. Student body president. President of my high school's National Honor Society. Summer student at a prestigious college preparatory/boarding school. The mid-South's first alternate to "Teenager of the Year." And the "Most Likely to Succeed" student in Northside High School's graduating class of 1982. All this while working a minimum of twenty hours a week at a family entertainment center and pizza restaurant—Chuck E. Cheese. I stayed away from the private part of myself that is just below the surface. The things I share with only my family and closest friends.

Chapter 5: Mind Games

I am certain he didn't want to hear about me, at eight years of age, staring down the barrel of a .38-caliber revolver under a white-knuckled death grip in my father's hand. The same gun, just a few years earlier, was pointed at him by my older brother. My brother, not merely pointing the gun but pulling the trigger. Or at twelve years of age, being beaten by my father until the blood drained from my face, making my lips essentially translucent. And the thoughts that raced through my mind afterwards. Should I recount the countless times my siblings and I soaked in a bathtub of Epsom salt to heal—but really to conceal—the wounds inflicted by Killer? No. He did not want to hear that. Those things stayed locked in a secure location in my mind. My mental vault. Let out only on special occasions.

I left the interview feeling good. Brian was easy to talk with and obviously very pro-Yale. He did a great job selling me on Yale. However, that was not necessary. I was already sold even before entering his home. The things that stood out most from the experience were playing ping-pong in his basement and the sheer amount of floor space throughout the house. Enough room to easily find a quiet corner or safe space if needed. I did come away with an understanding that I would hear from Yale within the next week or so regarding my application. The waiting game was almost over.

A few weeks later when I arrived home after my Friday-night shift at Chuck E. Cheese, I saw a letter from Yale in the stack of mail on the kitchen table. It was from the office of admissions. I was once again anxious and excited to open it but also apprehensive. I had already been accepted at several very good colleges, so I was certainly going to college. However, my desire was to go to Yale.

"Little Boo,"—my childhood nickname—"is that you?" "Yeah, mom. I hope I didn't wake you." "Oh no. I'm just relaxing and watching a movie. You have some mail on the kitchen table. I think there's a letter from Yale." "Thanks mom. I see it." I took the letter to my room. In case it was disappointing news, I would at least have some privacy to lick my wounds. I shut the door and took a deep breath. Closed my eyes and said a prayer.

"Dear Henry, Welcome to Yale College! It is with the greatest enthusiasm that I write to congratulate you on your admission to the Class of 1986."

Reflections

How has your mind helped or hurt you?

When was the last time you changed your mind on an important topic?

What mental work do you need to do?

PART III: WINNING WITH YOUR SOUL

For what shall it profit a man, if he shall gain the whole world, and lose his own soul?

—Mark 8:36 (KJV)

Chapter 6: Forgiveness

To forgive is to set a prisoner free and discover that the prisoner was you.

—Lewis B. Smedes

To err is human; to forgive, divine.

—Alexander Pope

When you forgive, you in no way change the past—
but you sure do change the future.

—Bernard Meltzer

She felt a weight pressing down on her. Was she awake or was this a dream? After all, she lived alone. She had been alone for years now. With her children all grown—at least eighteen years of age—she could enjoy some peace and quiet. After her youngest child received his high school diploma—something she herself was not able to do, ending her education after the eleventh grade—her job was done. Each child would now need to make his/her own way in the world.

Her mind started to make the transition from a sleep state to a conscious awareness. This was no dream. Someone was on top of her. Who? How? Had someone broken into her house? What the _ _ _ _ was going on? Then her memory kicked in.

When she had opened the door, the man said, "Mom. I have nowhere else to go." Every bone in her body told her not to let him in. But a mother cannot resist helping her child in need. She knew he was unstable—had been for years. His condition worsened if he was off his meds. Alternating between good mental health and a delusional paranoia that put everyone around him at risk. But what choice did she have. He had no one else.

As the realization of what was happening sunk in, she was bewildered. Repulsed. Saddened. But most of all, just plain angry. Angry at her disturbed son. Angry at the circumstances that brought him to her door. Angry at herself for allowing him into her home in the first place. She recognized the face above her, but it was not her son. There appeared to be no awareness of who she was. "Son!" she screamed. "What are you doing? I'm your mother. This is wrong."

Her voice and words seemed to have startled him. Or brought him back to his senses. If only for a moment. It was long enough. With all her strength, she pushed him aside. Leapt to her feet. And bolted out the door onto a deserted street. Leaving behind everything she owned—not concerned about the lack of clothing to shield her body. He did not pursue her.

I was in my junior year at Yale when I got the news. One of my siblings had called to inform me of the incident. I did not talk much during the conversation. I could not talk much. The thought was unthinkable. It made me sick—literally. The one thought that did make its way into my mind was my brother does not deserve to live. Anyone capable of committing such an act should be put to death. There is no place for them in a civilized world.

It would be several days before I could even think about talking to my mother. What would I say? What could I say? "Hi mom. How are you?" "Oh, I'm alright little Boo." Long silence. "I suppose you're calling about the incident with your brother," she said. We had not spoken in several months, maybe longer. That was not unusual. I was extremely busy at college with a very demanding major—electrical engineering, a very demanding sport—crew, and several part-time jobs. Mom had fourteen other living children to keep up with—having lost only one child, Rose Marie, shortly after childbirth. "Mom, what happened?" I managed to get out, choking back tears. Tears of sadness for the trauma she had undergone. Not just for this most recent incident, but for all the things my father had done to her. And now, to suffer abuse at the hands of a child was more than I could imagine.

Dee La recounted that horrible night. I listened with as much focus as I could muster. Fighting to keep my mind from drifting to the plans I had already started laying in place to deal with my brother. I listened not only to my mom's words but also to the way she said them. There was no anger in her voice, which was not altogether surprising. Mom was a very compassionate person. As the conversation went on, it became clear to me that she had forgiven my brother for this incredibly vile act. "Mom. I just don't

Chapter 6: Forgiveness

understand. How can you forgive him for what he did to you?" Silence. I could tell she was searching for the right words.

Finally, she spoke. "Little Boo, no thing and no one in this world is going to stop me from seeing Jesus. And you can't get to heaven with hatred in your heart. So, no matter what someone does to you, you have to forgive them. Now I have forgiven your brother. And you have to do the same." "But mom," I could not find the words to complete my thought. But I didn't need to. Mom knew where I was going. She interrupted, "You can't let this ruin your life. You are going to graduate from Yale University next year. And I am going to be there in the front row. I have spoken to your other brothers and told them the same thing. Don't do anything to your brother. Besides, you know he is not right in the head."

NO MATTER WHAT

Mom's words were still ringing in my ears two weeks later. "No matter what someone does to you, you have to forgive them." What if someone spat on me? Lied about me? Cheated on me? Stole from me? What if someone called me a Nigger? Killed—hung—my dog? Beat me? Shot me? What if someone raped me? I let the words "no matter what" sink in—*really* sink in.

What does it mean to forgive? And not just say the words, "I forgive you." But to truly forgive. Wikipedia tells us that "forgiveness, in a psychological sense, is the intentional and voluntary process by which one who may initially feel victimized, undergoes a change in feelings and attitude regarding a given offense, and overcomes negative emotions such as resentment and vengeance (however justified it might be)."[1]

When mom said, "Now I have forgiven your brother," was that what she meant? Truly. Completely. I concluded that she did. Where in the name of God had she gotten the strength to do that? And in my question, I found the answer. Like Jack Schwarz, she found it through the power of God. And in her case, more specifically, Jesus Christ. She believed her Savior—throughout the Holy Bible—had commanded her to forgive others so that she would be forgiven. Nowhere more directly than in Matt 6:12, in the Lord's Prayer: "And forgive us our debts, as we forgive our debtors" (KJV).

Her desire to spend eternity with her savior in heaven burned within her very being. It consumed her. Was a part of her. More familiar than every birthmark. Deeper than the lines in the palms of her hands. It allowed her

---

1. Wikipedia, "Forgiveness."

to see beyond the ugliness of this world. Accepting that this life is temporary, she was able to keep her eyes focused on something more appealing. Everlasting. Today's pain—no matter how severe—pales in comparison to an eternity of beauty and peace. But to experience that bliss, she had to find a way to forgive.

Did I have that type of desire? Or expectation of an afterlife that offered eternal happiness? I had been raised as a Christian, so I was certainly aware of heaven and hell—admittedly the Christian perception of each location. But, now at Yale exposed to people from different countries, I had become acquainted with other religious and nonreligious beliefs.

Growing up in Memphis, I had not encountered anyone who was not a Christian. At least not to my knowledge. The only diversity being the specific denomination of Christianity—Catholic, Eastern Orthodox, Protestant, or Independent Sacramental. Then within one of the major denominations, were you a Baptist, Anabaptist, Evangelical, Jehovah's Witness, Lutheran, Methodist, Mormon, Quaker, Seventh-Day Adventist, etc.? So, the question of whether heaven, hell, or God existed never came up. It was a bona fide fact—proven with the authority of the Holy Bible.

What was this strange new concept of coming back to life after you die? And possibly not even as a human being? Or on this planet? Who was Buddha? Or was it The Buddha? And who or what was Brahman? What if there was nothing at all after death?

With these foreign thoughts now rattling around in my head, naturally, I started to ask, Which one is right? But should I even be having these thoughts? Am I losing my faith by simply asking the question? But hold on. Isn't that precisely the point of college? To question things. Debate ideas. Find the truth. Or at least my truth. René Descartes said that "if you would be a real seeker after truth, it is necessary that at least once in your life you doubt, as far as possible, all things."[2]

So how do you find the truth about the afterlife—a subject that is off limits unless you are in a religious studies class or enrolled at a theological seminary? Broaching it could end friendships. Break family bonds. Spark physical confrontations between individuals. Or start wars between countries. Everyone knows what will happen to them when they die. Right? And if you suggest anything different from what they say, you are the enemy. Or an instrument of Satan—according to Christians—and too blind to see it. If you are talking to a Hindu or Buddhist, you are simply an unenlightened

---

2 Good Reads, "René Descartes."

Chapter 6: Forgiveness

being, who lacks self-awareness. An atheist would tell you that you are just stupid, gullible, or both if you believe there is anything after death. Probably the most rational response would come from an agnostic. We do not know, and some would say cannot know, what will happen to us after we die.

Every religion/nonreligion has its belief, and none can prove they are right. And conversely, no religion/nonreligion can prove that another religion/nonreligion is wrong. So, what are we to do? How do I find a desire—like mom—to spend eternity in a place that may or may not exist? If I were considering only Christianity, that would be straightforward. With only two choices, heaven (eternal goodness) and hell (eternal badness), of course I would desire heaven.

But as I dig beneath the surface, I discover that while spending eternity in heaven would be great, I am more concerned about spending eternity in hell. So, my true goal is to avoid a bad afterlife, rather than achieving a good one. For our purposes, good is defined as a condition the soul desires, providing a feeling or sense of pleasure, peace, comfort, and the like. Bad is defined as a condition the soul does not desire, providing a feeling or sense of pain, suffering, discomfort, and the like. And, as mentioned above, avoiding a bad condition—even if a good condition is not achieved—is also considered good. That is really my burning desire—regardless of which religion/nonreligion is being considered. We will explore these afterlife conditions in much more detail throughout the remainder of the book.

Chapter 7: Finding Desire

*Human behavior flows from three main sources:
desire, emotion, and knowledge.*

—Plato

*There are two tragedies in life. One is to lose your heart's desire.
The other is to gain it.*

—George Bernard Shaw

If I find in myself a desire which no experience in this world can satisfy, the most probable explanation is that I was made for another world.

—C. S. Lewis

Revisiting my talk—"The DNA of a Winner"—from the introduction, how do I find the sweet spot? Or at least for now, the first ingredient. Desire.

I start by following habit number two from Stephen R. Covey's *The 7 Habits of Highly Effective People*. "Begin with the End in mind."[1] An agnostic will advise that it is not possible to know what will happen to us before we die. This is both reasonable and logical since human beings do not know the future. Thus, each religious/nonreligious viewpoint has an equal probability of being correct. So, I look at "The End" for a human being according to each theology or ideology (see appendix A).

---

1. Covey, *7 Habits*, 95.

Chapter 7: Finding Desire

Then I ask myself, What would I desire if that specific afterlife possibility turned out to be the truth about what will happen to me when I die? An analysis of the top twenty-two major religions/nonreligions (as defined by Adherents.com) reveals that the fate of humans after their death is grouped into five afterlife possibilities. These beliefs account for over 98 percent of the world's population.

Before delving into the different afterlife possibilities, I make two key assumptions for discussion purposes. They factor into my subsequent analysis and decision-making process.

First, I assume that human beings have a soul (spirit, mind, consciousness, energy, force, etc.—whatever you call that part of a human being which survives physical death).

Most modern dictionaries define the soul as the spiritual or immaterial part of a human being. It is regarded as a distinct entity that exists separate from the body. The soul would be analogous to the software that runs your computer. When the software is installed, it is considered a part of the computer. However, the software exists separately from the computer. It can be uninstalled and transferred or downloaded onto another computer. Interestingly, numerous religions declare that the soul—like computer software—can be downloaded onto or into another human body or other material object once its current body is destroyed.

Second, I assume the human soul is immortal.

Now neither of these assumptions can be regarded as a fact. Nevertheless, we must assume their existence to have a reasonable and rational discussion regarding the fate of human beings after physical death. If human beings do not have a soul, then the whole discussion of the afterlife is meaningless, silly, and in fact a complete waste of time and energy.

And additionally, if the human soul is not immortal, then the question of what happens to it is also meaningless. Whether the soul existed on planet Earth or some other celestial body, would be irrelevant. It would not make a difference if it lived out its existence in another realm, dimension, or spirit world. The soul could have occupied many different bodies—human, animal, insect, or some other species. At some point, regardless of the number of years, rebirths, or reincarnations, it would simply vanish. Now our goal is to determine the soul's final fate—The End. What may happen to the soul between today and its ultimate destination is interesting but not our aim. As a result, if we knew for a fact the soul was not immortal, this book would end immediately. Full stop. Drop the mic.

However, since we must consider all possibilities to determine "The End" for a human being, both the existence and nonexistence of a soul are evaluated. And when the soul does exist, both a mortal and immortal soul are included in our discussion and analysis. In the case where the human soul is immortal, the soul's objective is to avoid a bad afterlife. That is every soul's burning desire, which is automatically achieved if humans do not have a soul. And the same holds true if the soul is mortal.

WITHOUT A TRACE

The first afterlife possibility is one where there is no form of life after death. Once we expire from the physical world, it is over. We disappear without a trace. Followers within the secular/nonreligious/agnostic/atheist, Chinese traditional religions (Chinese folk religions), African traditional and diasporic religions, and Unitarian Universalism (see appendix B) hold this belief.

In this afterlife scenario there is nothing after death. No heaven or hell. No new world. No in-between world. No reincarnation or rebirth onto this planet or any other astronomical body. No new universe. No union or reunion with God, the Supreme Being, the eternal spirit, or spiritual beings of any sort. No part of us continues to exist, which means that whether we have a soul is irrelevant, because it also ceases to exist once we die. We have no memory of our life on earth because we no longer have a memory, consciousness, or anything else. We simply vanish. Like a candle blown out, we disappear in every way.

If this were the reality of what awaits me after death, then I would have no future beyond the grave. This would naturally allow me, and everyone else, to achieve my desire—to avoid a bad afterlife.

DÉJÀ VU

The second afterlife possibility has no heaven and no hell. God(s) may or may not exist. The environment would be very much as it is today on Earth. Except it would be a purely spiritual world(s) instead of a physical one. Traditional Shinto calls the most sacred of these "the other world of heaven."

Followers within several religions, including secular/nonreligious/agnostic/atheist, Chinese traditional religions (Chinese folk religions), primal indigenous religions, African traditional and diasporic religions, Spiritism, neo-paganism, and Unitarian Universalism (see Appendix B), hold this view.

What the soul accomplishes in this spiritual world will determine if it has a good or bad afterlife. Recall our definitions of good and bad from chapter 6. Its perception of good and bad will also play a major role.

The soul's starting position would not be the dominant factor in determining if it ultimately has a good or bad afterlife. From our physical world, we know that an individual can start out in a bad condition and move into a good condition. The reverse is also true. This could happen suddenly by way of luck—good or bad—or through a lifetime of focused effort. Furthermore, whatever a person's current condition, it need not be permanent. It can change—from good to bad or bad to good—many times throughout a person's life. With eternity as the soul's life span, it is not only possible but probable that a soul's condition will change many times during its existence.

This spiritual afterlife reality offers the possibility of either condition for my soul. Naturally I would want a good existence. Attaining and maintaining a good afterlife—thus avoiding a bad afterlife—would be subjective. But most definitely desirable and achievable.

THE MERRY-GO-ROUND

The third afterlife possibility is centered around the concept of reincarnation, rebirth, or transmigration. All three terms, with some slight variations across cultures, involve the soul returning to the physical or natural world. For simplicity, I will use the term rebirth to represent all three terms going forward.

Now the soul is not actually reborn. For theologies that believe human beings have a soul, it is widely held that the soul is immortal. Therefore, it is not the soul that experiences death and rebirth. The soul simply moves from one host body to another. It is the host body that dies. When a new host body is born, the soul merges—or is downloaded like computer software—with it for its next life or incarnation. It is the same soul.

For our purposes, the physical or natural world refers to the entire universe. It encompasses all planets, moons, stars, objects, and matter of any kind. These ideologies incorporate the possibility that an individual could be reborn onto another planet or some other celestial body. Also included is allowance for the soul to be reborn into something other than a human body. It provides three potential outcomes.

Ain't No Stopping Us Now

In the first outcome, there is no escape from the cycle of birth, death, and rebirth. It continues forever. No soul ever gets off the merry-go-round. The soul continues to be reborn (or more accurately, attached to a new host body) for all eternity. Rebirth takes place in the physical or natural world. In the religious theologies that hold this belief, there is no world(s) other than the physical or natural living world. This living world does include other planets and astronomical bodies besides Earth. It spans the entire universe.

The religions that hold this belief—either entirely or a large subset of its followers—are Chinese traditional religions (Taoism—absent the Buddhist influence), primal-indigenous religions, African traditional and diasporic religions, and Tenrikyo (see appendix B).

In Tenrikyo, there is one exception for the founder of the religion, Nakayama Miki. She is also referred to as Oyasama by some followers. Her status is special. She is thought of as "everliving." Another point of differentiation is Tenrikyo's view on ending the cycle. True, there is no conclusive evidence that followers of Tenrikyo believe the cycle will ever end. Therefore, including it in this afterlife possibility is appropriate. However, some individuals within the religion do maintain that at the end of the existing creation—with a healthy dose of ambiguity about when that will be—all humans (souls) will receive salvation.

In this afterlife reality, there is no distinction between a good afterlife and a bad afterlife. It depends on your perspective. People in the Western Hemisphere generally view being reborn as good. People in the Eastern Hemisphere generally view it as bad. In either case, regardless of your perspective on its goodness or badness, every human would be destined to have the same fate. No exiting this world. As such, there is no "afterlife." And certainly, no bad afterlife—as we have defined it. This allows me, and everyone else, to achieve my desire.

Chapter 7: Finding Desire

Reunited, and It Feels So Good

In the second outcome, the cycle of birth, death, and rebirth does come to an end. It stops when the soul reaches a good place, a good state, or a reunion with God—covering all concepts of God. It embraces Brahman, the Supreme Being, the All That Is, kami, or any other notion of a universal God, spirit, energy, or force of nature. The religions that hold this belief—either entirely or a significant number of its followers—are Hinduism, Buddhism (encompassing Taoism, Shinto, and Cao Dai), primal indigenous religions, Sikhism, Spiritism, Jainism, neo-paganism, Unitarian Universalism, and Scientology (see appendix B).

In this afterlife reality—excluding Jainism and Shinto—all souls eventually reach the same destination. They gather in a good place, state, or reunion, often referred to as nirvana or moksha. If a human being does not reach this destination in his current lifetime, he will simply be reborn until he does. There is no limit to the number of times a soul is reborn. Sikhism teaches that there are 8.4 million species in the world. More recent estimates place the number slightly higher.

> "To date, a total of 1.3 million species have been identified and described, but the truth is that many more live on Earth. The most accurate census, conducted by the Hawaii's University, estimates that a total of 8.7 million species live on the planet."[2]

Whatever quantity is used as the exact number of species, the religion advocates that a soul will cycle through all species indefinitely until it is liberated.[3]

Like Sikhism, Jainism also teaches that each soul (with the closest Jain word being *jiva*, which means a conscious, living being) goes through 8.4 million—or 8.7 million if we use the most recent estimate—rebirths. The figure is most likely aligned with the number of species the religion considers to be on the planet.

However, unlike Sikhism, Jainism asserts that some souls can never attain liberation. This could be due to various reasons. It is generally the result of evil acts that have been committed. And while Sikhs believe all souls

---

2. Camps, "Biology."
3. RealSikhism, "Quotations > Reincarnation."

will eventually achieve liberation, the religion acknowledges—to some degree like Jainism—that if a person does not perform righteous deeds, his soul will stay in this endless loop. For these souls, they will continue in the cycle of birth, death, and rebirth forever. Their fate is included in the previously discussed afterlife reality—"The Merry-Go-Round: Ain't No Stopping Us Now."

In Shinto—absent the influence of Buddhism—the reunion of the human spirit/soul with the universal and eternal spirit (kami) is slightly different from the reunion envisioned by other religions in this group. Shinto has no concept of an eternal human spirit/soul. The spirit/soul also does not cycle through birth, death, and rebirth. Upon death, the person's spiritual energy—referred to as the soul in many religions—rejoins with kami. Kami is neither categorically good nor bad. It is simply the spiritual energy that resides in all living, and in some cases, nonliving things. Kami is capable of actions and activities that could be considered good or bad. For example, rain to a farmer experiencing a drought can be a welcomed sight—something very good. The same rain to a family at the base of a mountain facing a mudslide would be an unwelcomed potential disaster—something very bad. Since that part of a human being that survives physical death—irrespective of its name: soul, spirit, energy, force, consciousness, etc.—reunites with a universal and eternal spirit/energy, Shinto is appropriately included within this afterlife reality.

While Buddhism is also included in this afterlife reality, there are some unique aspects of the religion worth noting. At its foundation, Buddhism has a similar concept of God—kami—as Shinto. However, unlike Shinto, rebirth is a key component of Buddhism. Rebirth occurs due to karma generated in the individual's current or previous lives.

Another distinguishing feature of Buddhism—with similarities to Shinto—is the doctrine of anatta ("non-self"). It is regarded as one of the seven beneficial perceptions and one of the three marks of existence. "According to the anatta doctrine of Buddhism, at the core of all human beings and living creatures, there is no 'eternal, essential and absolute something called a soul, self or atman.' Buddhism, from its earliest days, has denied the existence of the 'self, soul' in its core philosophical and ontological texts."[4] Although absent a "personal" soul, Buddhism acknowledges that the essence within a human being does survive physical death. Think of it as an energy. And this essence or energy will continue to be reborn (or attached

---

4. Wikipedia, "Anattā."

Chapter 7: Finding Desire

to a new host body) until it is liberated. At which point it unites or reunites with the one eternal god/spirit/energy.

In some religions (Hinduism, Buddhism, Sikhism, Spiritism, and Jainism), the soul of a person who has committed evil acts will be sent to a bad place. Their stay is temporary until the soul is cleansed of or punished for the evil deeds or bad karma it has generated. The soul may be sent there in a natural cause and effect progression under its own power, or as a deliberate judgment by another being. In Hindu that being is Yama, the God of death, and the place is Naraka. Chinese Buddhism refers to the place as Diyu, with ten courts and multiple layers or stages. It is also presided over by the Hindu god Yama in Chinese mythology. Afterward, the soul is reborn. It continues in the cycle to death and then rebirth again until it is liberated and reaches nirvana, moksha, or a similar place/state.

Naturally, it may take some souls longer than others to reach this pure state, and therefore, they will have more experiences along their journey. Some of the experiences could be exceedingly good. Others could be exceedingly bad. All rebirths may not be onto planet Earth or into a human body.

For instance, Buddhism identifies six possible realms in which a soul can exist: the realm of gods, demi-gods, humans, animals, hungry ghosts, and hell.[5] The soul may or may not have an actual physical body, depending on the realm. In its next life, a soul may find itself on the moon, Jupiter, or some unknown celestial body.

The number of rebirths, locations within or outside the universe, and types of bodies that housed the soul is not a factor. It is reasonable to assume that all experiences along the way were necessary. They allowed the soul to reach maturity or enlightenment, then liberation, then nirvana, moksha, or a similar place/state. These existences were momentary stops along the highway leading to a permanent destination, which is our only concern. All religions within this group, except Spiritism and Scientology, teach that a person must rid himself of all karma—or at the very least, bad karma—to end the cycle.

The National Spiritualist Association of Churches does not espouse a belief of rebirth into the physical world. Spiritualists believe that upon death, the soul enters the spirit world. It lands at a level or realm based on the person's thoughts and actions during her lifetime on earth. The higher

---

5. Wikipedia, "Saṃsāra (Buddhism)."

the realm, the better the surroundings and conditions. Lower realms can have very unpleasant conditions.

Once in the spirit world, the soul will continue its progression upward within the realms—believed to be at least seven for humans—towards the Realms of the Light. Its level of attainment will depend on the soul's spiritual maturity or purity. Most souls will eventually reach the highest possible realm. However, any level above the second Realm of Light is considered good. And no soul is expected to end its progression at the first or second realm. Therefore, ending one's progression below the highest possible realm (i.e., anywhere between three and seven) results in a good afterlife.

Although the soul's progression is in the spirit world, Spiritism is appropriately included within this afterlife outcome. The soul departs the merry-go-round and ultimately ends the cycle in a good place. The potential to progress to higher levels of goodness within the spirit world is a bonus.[6]

The other religion which has a different approach to ending the cycle is Scientology. Scientology teaches that a soul, referred to as the thetan, must rid itself of psychic scars. The scars could have been inflicted over many lifetimes. The process to eliminate the scars is known as auditing. The auditor takes an individual, known as a PC or "preclear," through times in their life and claims to get rid of any past or current negative situations that may have a hold on to them. Once the scars are removed, the thetan is declared "clear." Cleared thetans then progress in spiritual maturity where they eventually become pure energy, thus ending the cycle of death, birth, and rebirth in a good state. A thetan will continue in the cycle indefinitely until this occurs. As a result, Scientology is most appropriately included within this afterlife reality.[7]

The group's remaining religions (Hinduism, Buddhism—encompassing Taoism, Shinto, and Cao Dai—primal indigenous religions, Sikhism, Jainism, neo-paganism, and Unitarian Universalism) focus on eliminating karma to end the cycle. There are various methods or paths to achieve the goal (see Hinduism and Buddhism in appendix B). As might be expected, the adherents from this group of religions believe that a follower of their specific religion will more easily and quickly reach this state. But nevertheless, they all assert that every human being will eventually reach this

---

6. National Spiritualist Association of Churches, "Religion."
7. Patheos, "Scientology."

Chapter 7: Finding Desire

state once they stop generating karma. And this becomes easier with each rebirth—so the theory goes.

The religions advocate that a soul continues its journey towards nirvana, moksha, or Sach Khand (The Realm of Truth) taking the lessons learned from the current life into the next one.[8] Within some of these religions, for example, Mahayana Buddhism and neo-paganism, the notion that a soul could continue its journey within the spiritual realm rather than the physical world is also taught.

The progression could take place in pleasant surroundings, often associated with the concept of heaven. Or it could be in a darker place, often associated with the concept of hell. The soul's journey is not dependent on the person's religious or nonreligious beliefs, but instead on his intentions, thoughts, words, and actions and resultant karma. His cumulative behaviors are driven by the lessons learned in previous lifetimes. One could be a Buddhist in this lifetime, a Christian in the next, an atheist in the following, and a Muslim in yet another. The soul simply continues its pursuit of ridding itself of karma whether in the physical world or the spiritual realm. If there is any punishment for bad karma or misdeeds from a previous lifetime, it is only temporary.

In some instances, bad or evil deeds are punished for a specific amount of time. The soul then reenters the cycle of birth, death, and rebirth where it continues its journey. Always striving for enlightenment that leads to liberation then nirvana, moksha, or a similar condition. In other cases, there is no punishment of any kind. If the individual has not been liberated, she is simply reborn.

Some religions argue that the soul continues its journey to enlightenment where it left off during its most recent life—after accounting for all merit personally gained or transferred to it. Others believe that the soul begins its journey anew with each life. Either way is acceptable. This is not a pertinent factor since we are concerned only with the soul's final fate and not how long it may take a soul to get there.

Another aspect of this afterlife reality we do not explore is the experiences a soul may have after death and before its next rebirth. As would be expected, there are numerous theories advanced by the religions that support the concept of rebirth.

Arguably one of the most detailed descriptions of the after-death experience in world literature is found in the Buddhist's text, *The Tibetan*

---

8. Sikhi Wiki. "Sach Kand."

Book of the Dead. The text outlines the soul's journey from death to rebirth. It includes an intermediate state that can last up to forty-nine days. During this forty-nine day period, the soul has several encounters. Again, in Buddhism, consciousness is the closest equivalent to the soul. Some of these encounters can involve frightening apparitions. How the soul responds to these situations determines its fate. It can achieve liberation, and be freed from the cycle of birth, death, and rebirth. Or it can stay on the merry-go-round and reenter the birth canal.[9] Here again either path is inconsequential. We are concerned only with the soul's final fate, which will be liberation. After which, it ends in a good place, a good state, or a reunion with God.

In this afterlife reality, there is only one possible outcome: a reunion with whatever you describe as God or simply a good place/state. As a result, my desire, along with everyone else, to avoid a bad afterlife would certainly be achieved.

Eraser

In the third outcome, the soul will depart the merry-go-round. It is provided with a limited number of attempts to end the cycle of birth, death, and rebirth through its own efforts. If the soul does not reach a good place, state, or reunion, it is destroyed by its creator or it simply vanishes. The Yarsan (within the primal-indigenous religions) holds this belief. Their assertion is that the soul has 1,001 rebirths to reach the good place (referred to as paradise by the Yarsan), state, or reunion.[10]

In this afterlife reality, the soul has either reached the good place, state, or reunion, or it has been extinguished. If extinguished, it could have been by a higher being or simply vanished under its own power. If it is in the good place, state, or reunion with God, it is of course experiencing a good afterlife. If it has been extinguished or vanished, one might conclude this outcome has resulted in a bad afterlife. However, that is not the case. For this soul it would be the same as if the soul is mortal.

Now, the soul would miss out on experiencing the goodness of heaven/paradise, some other blissful/peaceful state, or the reunion with God. But since the soul no longer exists, it would not know that or be able to appreciate or comprehend what it is missing out on. It could not be viewed as a

---

9. Padmasambhava, *Book of the Dead*, 217–304.
10. Hosseini, "Death in Yārsān."

punishment or undesirable condition by the soul. There would be no entity to accept the punishment or experience any harsh conditions. Once the soul disappeared, there would be nothing to have a memory, or association of any kind with its former existence. It would be as if the soul was never created. Therefore, if the soul was never created, it could not have a good or bad—recall our definitions of good and bad in chapter 6—afterlife. In fact, it would have no afterlife or any other type of existence to enjoy or regret.

If this were the reality of what awaits me after death, I of course would want to enjoy pleasant surroundings or dwell in the oneness with God for eternity. However, if I am not successful in this endeavor, then I (my soul) simply fades away with no lingering effects from my prior existence. There is no punishment and no bad place. Either outcome, in effect, results in a desirable afterlife. The absence of an afterlife cannot be considered a bad afterlife for the reasons discussed above. And avoiding a bad afterlife will have been achieved, which is my desire.

JUDGMENT DAY

The fourth afterlife possibility introduces the act of a final judgment. According to the religions that incorporate this belief into their theology, the judgment will be carried out in one of three ways:

1. The individual will be judged by her own thoughts, words, and deeds.
2. The individual will be judged by God, who is given many names: Exalted One and El Shaddai (Christianity), Allah (Islam), Jehovah and Yahweh (Judaism), Olorun (African traditional and diasporic religions), and many others.
3. The individual will be judged by Jesus Christ or by God through Jesus Christ.

In this afterlife, excluding Rastafarianism and some primal-indigenous religions, the soul is not reborn into the physical or natural world. You live once, you die, and then you are judged. No second chance. No do over.

Rastafarians (also referred to as Rastas) have a slight twist on this belief by incorporating the concept of reincarnation into their theology. They do believe in a single day of judgment, which is why they are included within this perspective of the afterlife. But until that day, all souls are reborn into the physical or natural world. Rebirth occurs immediately after death. Rastafarianism does not support the idea of any other worlds besides the physical or natural world. As such, Rastas maintain that heaven is literally on earth. It is identified, in general, as the continent of Africa and more specifically the country of Ethiopia.

All good or righteous souls will spend eternity in heaven (also called Jannah, Gan Eden, Orun Rere, and other names). For bad or unrighteous souls, there are three possible outcomes:

1. The soul is cleansed or purified, then enters heaven for eternity.
2. The soul is destroyed or extinguished.
3. The soul spends eternity in hell (also called Jahannam, Gehinnom, Orun Buru, and other names).

Some religions assert that the degree of reward a soul will receive in heaven or the degree of punishment in hell could vary. However, since there is universal agreement that heaven is a good place (i.e., a desirable condition) and hell is a bad place (i.e., an undesirable condition), we will not explore the degrees of goodness or badness within each place. Again, our focus is only to determine the soul's final resting place or state and not the shades of grey within the location/destination.

The good place could be one distinct location, an infinite number of places, or as many locations as there are human souls. In other words, each person or soul could have their very own unique good place. And the same could hold true for the bad place.

The religions that believe in a final judgment—either entirely or a significant number of its followers—are Christianity, Islam, primal-indigenous religious, African traditional and diasporic religions, Judaism, Bahá'í, Zoroastrianism, Unitarian Universalism, and Rastafarianism (see appendix B).

Control

As we turn to the three ways judgment could be administered, the first way advocates that the soul will be judged by the individual. It will be based on her own thoughts, words, and deeds—independent of her religious or nonreligious beliefs. This ideology is found within the Bahá'í religion.

In the Bahá'í faith, there is no external being that decides the soul's fate. Only what the person thought, said, and did while on Earth decides her fate. Based on these actions, the individual would develop a set of spiritual attributes: kindness, generosity, integrity, truthfulness, humility, and selfless service to others. These attributes or virtues will bolster her soul in the next life, which is purely spiritual.

The goal is to acquire as many spiritual attributes or virtues as possible. This will allow the soul to progress faster and from a higher level within the spirit world. Its destination is a spiritual purity that brings it close to God. It is this closeness to God that Bahá'ís refer to as heaven or paradise. Failure to develop the necessary attributes or virtues results in being apart or far from God. This state is considered hell.

Souls in the Bahá'í hell do not experience any deliberate torture or punishment inflicted by an external entity. Being apart or far from God and missing out on the bliss of this closeness is considered punishment enough.

Once in the spirit world, the soul begins its eternal progression towards God. The journey begins from the appropriate level its spiritual attributes or virtues dictated. There is no conclusive evidence that Bahá'ís believe every soul will attain the heaven-equivalent closeness to God. On one hand, Wikipedia indicates that "the Bahá'í writings state that the soul is immortal and after death it will continue to progress until it attains God's presence." On the other hand, the online encyclopedia acknowledges that sociologist researchers have observed that Bahá'ís have an inclusivistic belief that although it may take work, most [but not all] people will eventually be saved or get to heaven."[11]

If this were the reality of what awaits us after death, then failure to achieve a closeness with God would result in a bad afterlife. Naturally, my desire would be to enjoy the benefits bestowed by an intimate relationship with God. However, in this afterlife, a bad outcome is equally likely as a good one. So, I, as is the case with every human being, would have the opportunity to achieve my desire. But no guarantee.

The Scales of Justice

In the second way the judgment is carried out, the individual will be judged by God. The religions that subscribe to this ideology are Islam, African traditional and diasporic religions, Judaism, Zoroastrianism, Unitarian Universalism, and Rastafarianism.

---

11. Wikipedia, "Bahá'í Faith."

The judgment is predicated on the individual's foundational belief in God, that he, she, or it does indeed exist and will exercise judgment on all souls. A person who does not believe in a God that passes judgment is viewed as not fearing or, said another way, not respecting God, shunning God, or turning away from righteousness. Without this belief, the person's soul will be sent to hell, irrespective of their deeds.

The criteria or yardstick God will use varies amongst these religions. In general, it will be a balancing or weighing of good deeds or righteous acts against bad/evil deeds (encompassing intentions, thoughts, words, and actions). If your good deeds outweigh your bad deeds, you go to heaven. If your bad deeds outweigh your good deeds, you go to hell.

Within some of the religions, there is an intermediate or in-between place if your good and bad/evil deeds are weighed equally. It can also be the place where the soul goes to be purified or punished for its bad/evil deeds. In the Roman Catholic Christian denomination this place is known as purgatory and as Sheol or Gehinnom in some Jewish traditions.

All religions that believe in such a place advocate that the soul's tenure is only temporary in this location. Once the soul is cleansed of its bad/evil deeds or the soul is credited with enough additional good deeds to tip the scales, it then proceeds to heaven for the rest of eternity. A soul can acquire more good deeds through numerous methods. According to Catholics, a soul can gain merit from another individual's abundance of good deeds or from prayers by those still alive. Other religions promote different approaches, culminating in the same outcome. All good souls eventually go to heaven.

To determine a bad soul's final resting place, we need to revisit the three potential outcomes postulated by the religions that subscribe to the belief of a final judgment. Again, this only applies to individuals who believed in the existence of a God who will pass judgment on souls for their actions while they were alive on earth. Those who did not are sent straight to hell, where their soul could be tormented for all eternity.

Purified

In the first potential outcome, the bad soul is purified, then sent to heaven for eternity. There is no consensus on where the soul's purification takes place (hell, purgatory, the Bardo, or some other locale) or how long the purification process takes (a day, a month, a year, a million years, or more).

Chapter 7: Finding Desire

However, since we are only interested in the final fate of the soul, all opinions are acceptable, rendering these questions insignificant and irrelevant to our discussion.

If this were the reality of the judgment day afterlife, every soul that believed in a God that passes judgment enjoys a good afterlife, thus, fulfilling their heart's desire.

Destroyed

In the second potential outcome, the bad soul is destroyed or extinguished. At first glance, it appears this outcome would result in a bad afterlife for some souls even if they believed in a judging God. However, upon closer examination, that is not the case. For these souls it would be the same as if the soul was not immortal.

Now the soul would miss out on experiencing the goodness of heaven. But since the soul no longer exists, it would not know that or be able to appreciate or comprehend what it is missing out on. It could not be viewed as an undesirable condition by the soul since there would be nothing or no one to accept the punishment. Once the soul was destroyed, it would have no memory or association of any kind with its former existence. It would be as if the soul was never created. Now if the soul was never created, it could not have a good or bad—recall our definitions of good and bad in chapter 6—afterlife. In fact, it would have no afterlife or any other type of existence to enjoy or regret.

If this were the reality of what awaits me after death, I of course would want to enjoy the pleasantries of heaven for eternity. However, if I am not successful in this endeavor, then I (my soul) simply fades away with no lingering effects from my prior existence. There is no punishment and no bad place. Either outcome, in effect, results in a desirable afterlife. The absence of an afterlife is not the same as a bad afterlife for the reasons stated above. And avoiding a bad afterlife will have been achieved, which is my desire.

Punished

In the third potential outcome, the bad soul is sent to hell for a horrible and undesirable eternal existence. Even if we believed in a God who passes judgment, our deeds—encompassing intentions, thoughts, words, and actions—will seal our fate. If this were the reality of the judgment day afterlife, then I would want to do everything humanly possible to avoid this outcome. However, a bad afterlife is a possibility even for individuals who believed in a judging God. So, there is no guarantee I will achieve my desire.

The Lion and the Lamb

We conclude our discussion of the ways the judgment could be administered with the third way. Here the individual will be judged by Jesus Christ or by God through Jesus Christ. The only religion that subscribes to this ideology is Christianity.

Christians believe that our path to a good afterlife goes through Jesus Christ. It is not based on a judgment or balancing of our deeds (encompassing intentions, thoughts, words, and actions). The criteria Jesus will use hinges on our belief about who he is. In Matt 16:13–17 "[Jesus] asked his disciples, 'Who do people say the Son of Man is?' They replied, 'Some say John the Baptist; others say Elijah; and still others, Jeremiah or one of the prophets.' 'But what about you?' he asked. 'Who do you say I am?' Simon Peter answered, 'You are the Messiah, the Son of the living God.'" Jesus goes on to say, "Blessed are you, Simon son of Jonah, for this was not revealed to you by flesh and blood, but by my Father in heaven" (NIV).

Believing that Jesus Christ is the Son of God is a foundational requirement, but Christianity also teaches that you must act on this belief. The most important acts are described in Rom 10:9, which states, "If you declare with your mouth, 'Jesus is Lord,' and believe in your heart that God raised him from the dead, you will be saved" (NIV).

Let me pause here for a minute to reflect on the phrasing in this statement around the word believe. What does it mean to "believe in your heart"? What if you only believe in your mind but not in your heart? You know. The kind of pseudo belief that does not have any actions behind it. That is not the kind of belief referred to here. Your belief must be genuine, where you absolutely think—and feel—your belief is the truth. A Google search returns the following definition of the word believe: "accept (something) as true; feel sure of the truth of."[12]

Having your belief confirmed as the truth is not the requirement. But only that you think it is true and act in accordance with that belief. Now this is not to suggest that individuals' actions always align perfectly with

12. *Oxford Languages*, "Believe."

Chapter 7: Finding Desire

their beliefs. Attempting to understand the reasons why this occurs is beyond the scope of this book. Furthermore, determining whether the belief an individual professes is truly in his heart is beyond the ability of human beings. That is between the person and God—if he, she, or it exists.

Now let's get back to this final judgment day scenario.

The Christian Holy Scriptures further document how the judgment will be carried out for an individual who has not completed these acts. In Matt 10:32–33, Jesus states, "Whoever acknowledges me before others, I will also acknowledge before my Father in heaven. But whoever disowns me before others, I will disown him before my Father in heaven" (NIV).

And finally, the Christian Bible asserts that there is no other way to God except through Jesus Christ. In John 14:6, when questioned about the place he was preparing for his followers and how to get there, Jesus answered his disciple Thomas by saying, "I am the way and the truth and the life. No one comes to the Father except through me" (NIV).

If this were the reality of the judgment day afterlife, then how we live our lives while on earth most certainly matters. In addition to a belief in a judging God, we must verbally acknowledge that Jesus Christ is Lord—the Son of God—and believe in our heart that God raised him from the dead to be the Savior of the world. Only by completing these acts can we gain admittance into heaven and enjoy a good afterlife. Failure to meet these foundational requirements will cause us to be sentenced to hell for all eternity. Christianity is the only religion that holds to this teaching. Therefore, in this afterlife reality, only Christians will go to the good place (heaven). All others will go to the bad place (hell or the lake of fire in some Christian traditions) for all eternity. A fate I desperately want to avoid, with a burning desire.

DECISION DAY

The fifth, and final, afterlife possibility is not one that is promoted—at least not directly—by any of the religions in appendix A. One possible exception being Juche. Juche advocates that man is the master of everything and decides everything; so, whatever happens after death will be decided by man. This ideology does not have an "official" following and does not receive serious debate among religious scholars. However, it has garnered the attention of many Gen X, millennial, and Generation Z individuals. At the heart of this afterlife possibility is the belief that the individual creates her own reality—in life and in death.

If indeed this could be achieved, it would mean that each person decides their afterlife fate. Either prior to or after death, the person would choose the type of afterlife they would enjoy. The ability to choose is not granted because of how we lived our lives while on earth. The decision point is not taken away based on our actions/deeds, whether good or bad. We also do not lose the ability to choose due to our beliefs, ideologies, self-awareness, or level of spiritual awakening. These things simply have no bearing on the option we have been granted.

If this were the reality of what awaits us after death, then every human would have the ability to choose a good afterlife. It would be according to their wishes. And with avoiding a bad eternal existence at the top of the list, they would achieve their heart's desire.

AND THE WINNER IS

Note: In the following analysis, the word religion includes those ideologies that may be referred to as a nonreligion.

The table below summarizes the probability of an individual achieving his desire—avoiding a bad afterlife. It determines the fate of an individual's soul—for each of the twenty-two religions/nonreligions—in each of the five afterlife possibilities. As stated earlier, the perspective that human beings have an immortal soul is implicit in the analysis.

Afterlife Possibility	Religion	Probability of achieving the desired afterlife
Without a Trace	Every religion	100%
Déjà Vu	Every religion	50%
The Merry-Go-Round: Ain't No Stopping Us Now	Every religion	100%
The Merry-Go-Round: Reunited, and It Feels So Good	Every religion	100%
The Merry-Go-Round: Eraser	Every religion	100%

Chapter 7: Finding Desire

Afterlife Possibility	Religion	Probability of achieving the desired afterlife
Judgment Day: Control	Every religion	50%
Judgment Day: The Scales of Justice, Purified	God-fearing religion	100%
Judgment Day: The Scales of Justice, Purified	Non-God-fearing religion	0%
Judgment Day: The Scales of Justice, Destroyed	God-fearing religion	100%
Judgment Day: The Scales of Justice, Destroyed	Non-God-fearing religion	0%
Judgment Day: The Scales of Justice, Punished (Islam)	God-fearing religions except Christianity, Hinduism, Chinese folk religions, some African traditional and diasporic religions, Cao Dai	50%
Judgment Day: The Scales of Justice, Punished (Islam)	Non-God-fearing religions, Christianity, Hinduism, Chinese folk religions, some African traditional and diasporic religions, Cao Dai	0%
Judgment Day: The Scales of Justice, Punished (African traditional and diasporic religions)	God-fearing religion	50%
Judgment Day: The Scales of Justice, Punished (African traditional and diasporic religions)	Non-God-fearing religion	0%
Judgment Day: The Scales of Justice, Punished (Judaism)	God-fearing religion	50%
Judgment Day: The Scales of Justice, Punished (Judaism)	Non-God-fearing religion	0%
Judgment Day: The Lion and the Lamb	Christianity	100%
Judgment Day: The Lion and the Lamb	Every religion except Christianity	0%
Decision Day	Every religion	100%

By averaging the probabilities assigned to each religion, we find that Christianity offers its followers the best chance of achieving their desire. With a 76.92 percent probability (see appendix C), it is 67 percent greater than religions that do not acknowledge the existence of a God who passes judgment on human souls. In determining whether a religion acknowledges this type of God, I have used a broad definition of the word judgment. If the religion indicates that God will participate—whether directly or indirectly—in affecting the soul's ultimate destination, it has been included.

This is not to say that Christianity is "right," and all other religions are "wrong." As agnostics correctly point out, no one knows what will happen to us after we die. Therefore, the question of which religion is "right" cannot be determined. Christianity is simply the most reasonable, logical, and rational choice. It offers the greatest reward—achieving the desired afterlife in all afterlife possibilities—with the least amount of risk in relation to all other beliefs.

Let's bring this down to the individual's level in a head-to-head comparison. We compare the fate of individuals from other faiths with that of a Christian. This is assessed using each religion's belief of what comes next and the probability of achieving one's desire in both religions' afterlife reality. Let's look at three examples. We begin with an atheist.

Atheism teaches that there is no God and no afterlife—captured in the "Without a Trace" afterlife possibility. Christianity advocates there is a God with his Son, Jesus Christ, and an afterlife. In the Christian afterlife Jesus Christ—or God through Jesus Christ—will judge all human souls. This perspective is captured in the afterlife possibility "Judgment Day: The Lion and the Lamb."

For an atheist, if the atheist afterlife possibility turns out to be the truth, then there is nothing after death. Therefore, his desire—to avoid a bad afterlife—is achieved. If the Christian afterlife possibility turns out to be the truth, then he cannot achieve his desire. He will be tormented in hell (or the lake of fire) for all eternity. This equates to a 50 percent probability of achieving his desired afterlife.

For a Christian, if the atheist afterlife possibility turns out to be the truth, then there is nothing after death. Therefore, his desire—to avoid a bad afterlife—is achieved. If the Christian afterlife possibility turns out to be the truth, then his desire is also achieved. He will spend eternity in heaven. This equates to a 100 percent probability of achieving his desired afterlife.

Chapter 7: Finding Desire

Viewed from another perspective, an atheist has nothing to gain if he is right and everything to lose if he is wrong. On the other hand, a Christian has everything to gain if he is right and nothing to lose if he is wrong. This is a no-win situation for the atheist. Either outcome fails to benefit him in any way. In other words, an atheist wagering against a Christian is a fool's bet. Put in monetary terms, both the Christian and atheist bet one dollar (their soul). The Christian will either get his one dollar back or win one billion dollars (eternity in heaven). The atheist will either get his one dollar back or owe one billion dollars (eternity in hell/the lake of fire).

"For the wisdom of this world is foolishness in God's sight" (1 Cor 3:19 NIV). It is completely counterintuitive. What you would expect to receive in a traditional risk and reward transaction is turned upside down. When you take on more risk, you expect a higher reward if you win as compensation for the increased risk. Now in this situation comparing the afterlife belief of an atheist with that of a Christian, it is clear the atheist is taking more risk. Yet the reward/payout for an atheist—when he is correct and "wins"—is no more than the reward/payout for a Christian who would be wrong and "lose" in this afterlife reality.

And now let's look at the situation from the Christian perspective. When you take on less risk, you expect a lower reward if you win due to the decreased risk—the trade-off for "playing it safe." Again, in this situation, it is clear the Christian is taking less risk. Yet the reward/payout for a Christian is equal to or greater than the reward/payout for an atheist who assumes significantly more risk. Go figure.

Now an atheist might disagree. Claiming that he does gain something if he is correct. His reward is being able to live life on his own terms and benefiting from the satisfaction that comes with that. And to some extent the seventeenth-century French mathematician, physicist, inventor, philosopher, writer, and Catholic theologian Blaise Pascal might agree.

In his famous wager, Pascal concludes that a rational person should always bet on God's existence. He "proved" this mathematically using decision theory. Pascal argued that a bet against God's existence has a finite gain (one lifetime of pleasure on earth) with an infinite loss (eternity of torment in hell/the lake of fire). And a bet for God's existence has a finite loss (one lifetime of sacrifice on earth) with an infinite gain (eternity of peace and happiness in heaven). Implicit in his analysis are several assumptions that cannot be taken as facts. He assumes that humans are not reincarnated, hell is eternal, heaven is eternal, and there is no possibility of moving from hell to heaven or vise versa.[13]

Accepting his assumptions for the purpose of this discussion, I agree with Pascal's conclusion. However, he—ironically, like the atheist—overstates the gain (one lifetime of pleasure on earth) that would be received in a bet against God's existence. For an individual to be satisfied or receive any benefit from how he lived his life, he would have to look back on his life—his complete life—and be content. The gain would also have to be sustained. Permanent. And it would need to yield a net positive outcome while accounting for all positive and negative actions/results. At some point in our lives, most of us have undoubtedly been presented with a question like, "Looking back, knowing what you know now, would you have done anything differently?"

This question can only be answered—truly answered—at the end of our existence. At death. But to be more accurate, it would have to be after death. However, for now, we will equate our existence with our physical life. Atheists contend that science has proven there is no such thing as an afterlife.

In *The God Delusion*, Richard Dawkins lays out a logical and rational argument of how science can explain essentially all phenomenon. Dawkins, like most atheists, rejects the notion of any supernatural agency at work within or outside our universe. He leans heavily on the premise that knowledge is gained from observation, experience, and experimentation. We can test and gather quantifiable data to prove the truth of a theory or assertion. Then at the end of the book, he states that "as many atheists have said better than me, the knowledge that we have only one life should make it all the more precious."[14] What? Wait a second. Where is the quantifiable data that allows us to turn the theory or assertion that "we have only one life" into a fact? To his credit, Dawkins does begin the section "Inspiration" with the following admission: "This is a matter of taste or private judgement, which has the slight unfortunate effect that the method of argument I must employ is rhetoric rather than logic."[15]

But even if there was an afterlife, atheists would argue that it was meaningless or irrelevant. They base this assertion on the theory that human beings do not have a soul (spirit, mind, consciousness, energy, force,

---

13. Wikipedia, "Pascal's Wager."
14. Dawkins, *God Delusion*, 404–5.
15. Dawkins, *God Delusion*, 404.

Chapter 7: Finding Desire

etc.—whatever you call that part of a human being which survives physical death). This of course is a leap of faith, or to use Dawkins' terminology, another rhetorical argument.

As demonstrated in *Gambling With Your Soul*, "to know something is to know the truth—an absolute fact."[16] A fact can be proven with objective, verifiable evidence. Is it a fact that human beings have a soul? Is it a fact that human beings do not have a soul? The answer to both questions is no. An answer of no to one question does not infer an answer of yes to the other question. Independently, there are compelling arguments by renowned philosophers, scientists, and theologians supporting an affirmative yes for each question. However, there is no objective, verifiable evidence that can be presented for either question to render the answer as a fact. Naturally not everyone agrees with my statement.

Dr. Jim Tucker is likely one of those individuals. Dr. Tucker is the director of the Division of Perceptual Studies at the University of Virginia's School of Medicine. For the past twenty years, he has studied hundreds of cases where young children claimed to have memories of past lives. While occurrences have been reported worldwide, Dr. Tucker has focused mainly on the United States. In his book *Return to Life*, he documents many American cases, including those of James Leininger and Ryan Hammons. Both children had verifiable memories of past lives. Leininger had been a WWII pilot and Hammons had been a Hollywood extra and talent agent.[17]

While this is certainly compelling evidence, it has limitations. The evidence is only for the specific individuals involved. It confirms that some part of them (soul, spirit, mind, consciousness, energy, force, etc.) survived physical death. If we accept this as factual data, and therefore the truth, we can't generalize it to all humanity. We can't conclude that all humans will have or have had the same experience. Let's generously assume that one hundred million individuals alive at this moment have had this type of experience. That equates to only about 1.25 percent of the eight billion people in the world today.

Therefore, neither scenario can be removed from our decision-making process to determine what we ultimately choose to believe. And they both have the same probability of being correct, 50 percent. But for now, let's go with atheism's position that a human being does not have a soul or anything else that continues after death.

---

16. Davis, *Gambling*, 42.
17. Tucker, *Return to Life*, 63–119.

So, if no part of us survives physical death, then it would be impossible for an atheist to look back over his life. He would not be able to receive any satisfaction or benefit from how he lived his life. Of course, this does not eliminate the immediate joys or disappointments that would be experienced with each decision during the person's life. But regardless of the highs or lows the impact would be temporary. Occurring within his current lifetime with no lasting benefit to the individual.

And this includes a final review of his life while on his death bed, before taking his final breath. In a fraction of a second after his last breath, all the memories, feelings, accomplishments, and emotions—good or bad—that ran through his mind and body would instantly vanish. We're purposefully leaving out of the discussion any impact—positive or negative—he may have had on other individuals, society, or the world at large. Those results are irrelevant since he will never know the outcomes. Therefore, there is nothing the individual gains if the atheist afterlife possibility turns out to be the reality. This also confirms for the Christian there is nothing to lose if he is wrong in his view of the afterlife.

Another "gain" sometimes put forth by the atheist is not experiencing disappointment after getting his hopes up. He avoids the emotional letdown associated with believing in God's existence and discovering there is no God—and by extension, no heaven. Underlying atheism's philosophy is an implied correlation that if there is no God, then there is no afterlife. Which, of course, is not necessarily the case. But let's set that aside.

This might make you scratch your head. Since an individual can only discover the truth of what awaits him after his physical death, he cannot be disappointed with his belief while he is alive. He would be disappointed after he died if what he believed while alive turned out not to be the truth. So, a Christian would have lived his life with the hope of going to heaven and spending eternity in a place of beauty and peace with God. If it turns out this is not what awaits him after death, and in fact, there is nothing after death—or he does not have a soul—he will never know that God or heaven does not exist. He will also never know that he had lived his life in hopes of their existence. So, if the atheist afterlife possibility turns out to be correct, how could a Christian—or anyone for that matter—ever be disappointed with what they believed while they were alive? When would the disappointment be experienced? Never.

Now for the atheist, he would have lived his life with the expectation that there is nothing after his physical death. He believed he would cease

Chapter 7: Finding Desire

to exist with no connection to his former life. No consequences from his deeds (encompassing words, thoughts, and actions). And no continuing consciousness or experiences of any kind. If it turns out this is not what awaits him after death, and in fact, he has a soul, there is a God, Jesus Christ, heaven, and hell . . . oops. So, if the Christian afterlife possibility turns out to be correct, will the atheist experience disappointment? Absolutely. In fact, to avoid the possibility of being disappointed, one would want to be a Christian instead of an atheist. As Arsenio Hall and C+C Music Factory would say, this is one of those "Things That Make You Go Hmmm . . . "

We next consider the fate of a Buddhist with that of a Christian. Buddhism teaches that the soul—with the closest equivalent in Buddhism being consciousness—cycles through birth, death, and rebirth indefinitely until it reaches nirvana. Nirvana is a transcendent state of perfect peace and happiness. It is the equivalent of salvation for the soul referred to in other religions. This is the fate of all souls captured in the "Merry-Go-Round: Reunited, and It Feels So Good" afterlife possibility.

For a Buddhist, if the Buddhist afterlife possibility turns out to be the truth, then she will eventually reach nirvana. Therefore, her desire—to avoid a bad afterlife—is achieved. If the Christian afterlife possibility turns out to be the truth, then she cannot achieve her desire. She will be tormented in hell/lake of fire for all eternity. This equates to a 50 percent probability of achieving her desired afterlife.

For a Christian, if the Buddhist afterlife possibility turns out to be the truth, then she will eventually reach nirvana. Therefore, her desire—to avoid a bad afterlife—is achieved. If the Christian afterlife possibility turns out to be the truth, then her desire is also achieved. She will spend eternity in heaven. This equates to a 100 percent probability of achieving her desired afterlife.

As in the previous comparison between an atheist and a Christian, a Buddhist has nothing to gain if she is right and everything to lose if she is wrong. On the other hand, a Christian has everything to gain if she is right and nothing to lose if she is wrong. This is a no-win situation for the Buddhist. Either outcome fails to benefit her in any way. In other words, a Buddhist wagering against a Christian is a fool's bet. Put in monetary terms, both the Christian and Buddhist bet one dollar (their soul). The Christian will win one billion dollars (nirvana or eternity in heaven) in either afterlife reality. The Buddhist will either win one billion dollars (nirvana) or owe one billion dollars (eternity in hell/the lake of fire).

"For the wisdom of this world is foolishness in God's sight" (1 Cor 3:19 NIV). It is completely counterintuitive. What you would expect to receive in a traditional risk and reward transaction is again turned upside down. When you take on more risk, you expect a higher reward if you win, as compensation for the increased risk. Now in this situation comparing the afterlife belief of a Buddhist with that of a Christian, it is clear the Buddhist is taking more risk. Yet the reward/payout for a Buddhist—when she is correct and "wins"—is no more than the reward/payout for a Christian who would be wrong and "lose" in this afterlife reality.

And now let's look at the situation from the Christian perspective. When you take on less risk, you expect a lower reward if you win due to the decreased risk—the trade-off for "playing it safe." Again, in this situation, it is clear the Christian is taking less risk. Yet the reward/payout for a Christian is equal to or greater than the reward/payout for a Buddhist—who assumes significantly more risk. Go figure.

Now a Buddhist might disagree. Claiming that she does gain something if she is correct. Her reward. Being able to live a peaceful and fulfilling life eliminating all aspects of personal suffering. She, her soul, would receive the satisfaction from a stress-free existence. Yet, as revealed earlier, "According to the anatta doctrine of Buddhism, at the core of all human beings and living creatures, there is no 'eternal, essential and absolute something called a soul, self or atman.' Buddhism, from its earliest days, has denied the existence of the 'self, soul' in its core philosophical and ontological texts."[18] Although absent a "personal" soul, Buddhism acknowledges that the essence within a human being does survive physical death. Think of it as an energy. And this essence or energy will continue to be reborn (or attached to a new host body) until it is liberated. At which point it unites or reunites with the one eternal god/spirit/energy.

To achieve this perfect state of peace, the person must stop generating karma. And to do that requires eliminating all attachments. Thoughts, feelings, sensations, emotions, experiences, memories. The very things that make them human. Make them individuals. This is not a gain for the person, since there would be nothing remaining of the "person." It is simply a realization and acceptance of the fact that there was never an "individual" to begin with. This essence or energy that was in the physical body was always a part of the overall whole. Picture it as a piece in a jigsaw puzzle. It was momentarily detached, but it was always a part of the entire puzzle.

18. Wikipedia, "Anattā."

Chapter 7: Finding Desire

It was held accountable for its behaviors—karma—for a finite amount of time, until all karma was eliminated. Once that occurred, the essence or energy was liberated from the cycle of birth, death, and rebirth. It then reunited with the one eternal god/spirit/energy. The piece was placed back into the whole jigsaw puzzle. Reinserted with no individuality or recollection of ever being apart from it.

So, if we do not have an individual soul, then it would be impossible for a Buddhist—or anyone for that matter—to receive any personal satisfaction from how she lived her life. Of course, this does not eliminate the immediate joys or disappointments that would be experienced with each decision during the person's life. But regardless of the highs or lows the impact would be temporary. Occurring within her current lifetime, or cycles of lifetimes. There would be no lasting benefit to the non-existent individual soul. The Buddhist gains nothing if her afterlife possibility turns out to be the reality. This also confirms for the Christian, there is nothing to lose if she is wrong in her view of the afterlife.

We conclude by considering the fate of a Bahá'í with that of a Christian. The Bahá'í religion teaches that a person will be judged by their own thoughts, words, and deeds. After death, the soul enters the spirit world and begins its progression towards God. Achieving a closeness to God is considered heaven. Being apart from God is hell. Souls in the Bahá'í hell do not experience any deliberate torture or punishment inflicted by an external entity. Being apart or far from God and missing out on the bliss of this closeness is considered punishment enough. It is just as likely that a soul will attain this closeness as it is the soul will not. This perspective is captured in the afterlife possibility "Judgment Day: Control."

For a Bahá'í, if the Bahá'í afterlife possibility turns out to be the truth, then he has an equal chance of achieving a good or a bad afterlife. Therefore, his desire—to avoid a bad afterlife—is not assured. If the Christian afterlife possibility turns out to be the truth, then he cannot achieve his desire. He will be tormented in hell/the lake of fire for all eternity. This equates to a 25 percent probability of achieving his desired afterlife.

For a Christian, if the Bahá'í afterlife possibility turns out to be the truth, then he has an equal chance of achieving a good or a bad afterlife. Therefore, his desire—to avoid a bad afterlife—is not assured. If the Christian afterlife possibility turns out to be the truth, then his desire is achieved. He will spend eternity in heaven. This equates to a 50 percent probability of achieving his desired afterlife.

Viewed from another perspective, a Bahá'í has no upside against a Christian if he is right and a tremendous downside if he is wrong. On the other hand, a Christian has no downside against a Bahá'í if he is wrong and a tremendous upside if he is right. This is a no-win situation for the Bahá'í. In other words, a Bahá'í wagering against a Christian is a fool's bet. Put in monetary terms, both the Christian and Bahá'í bet one dollar (their soul). The Christian will either get his one dollar back (Bahá'í hell with no inflicted punishment) or win one billion dollars (Bahá'í closeness to God or eternity in heaven). The Bahá'í will either get his one dollar back (Bahá'í hell with no inflicted punishment), win one billion dollars (Bahá'í closeness to God), or owe one billion dollars (eternity in hell/the lake of fire).

"For the wisdom of this world is foolishness in God's sight" (1 Cor 3:19 NIV). It is completely counterintuitive. What you would expect to receive in a traditional risk and reward transaction is once again turned upside down. When you take on more risk, you expect a higher reward if you win, as compensation for the increased risk. Now in this situation comparing the afterlife belief of a Bahá'í with that of a Christian, it is clear the Bahá'í is taking more risk. Yet the reward/payout for a Bahá'í—when he is correct and "wins"—is no more than the reward/payout for a Christian who would be wrong and "lose" in this afterlife reality.

And now let's look at the situation from the Christian perspective. When you take on less risk, you expect a lower reward if you win due to the decreased risk—the trade-off for "playing it safe." Again, in this situation, it is clear the Christian is taking less risk. Yet the reward/payout for a Christian is equal to or greater than the reward/payout for a Bahá'í who assumes significantly more risk. Go figure.

This head-to-head comparison between religions reinforces the logic underpinning the analysis in appendix C. Each of the twenty-two religions is contrasted with the other twenty-one religions—in relation to the afterlife possibilities identified earlier in this chapter. The conclusion is clear. My desire is to avoid a bad afterlife, regardless of the religion/nonreligion that turns out to be the truth. And Christianity gives me the best chance at achieving that desire.

So, the obvious question is, How do I become a Christian?

Chapter 8: Forging Ability

Adversity causes some men to break; others to break records.
—William Arthur Ward

I've learned that fear limits you and your vision. It serves as blinders to what may be just a few steps down the road for you. The journey is valuable, but believing in your talents, your abilities, and your self-worth can empower you to walk down an even brighter path. Transforming fear into freedom—how great is that?
—Soledad O'Brien

I know of no more encouraging fact than the unquestionable ability of man to elevate his life by conscious endeavor.
—Henry David Thoreau

IN THE LAST CHAPTER, we solved for desire—the first ingredient to reach the sweet spot. Where winners live. We now tackle the second ingredient—ability. This one is a bit more complicated. Especially on the subject at hand. How to become a Christian if you are not already one. It will challenge the very foundation of who you are. At some point in our lives we have all been asked questions like, Who are you? What makes you tick? If not by another person, then we have probably asked ourselves in a quiet moment, Who am I?

If you were being interviewed for a job, you would likely start by stating where you went to school, in which branch of the military you served, or what jobs you have held. You may talk about some of your accomplishments. You would elaborate on your strengths, being sure to cover both the hard and soft skills that make you an ideal candidate for the job. If you are feeling brave or comfortable, you may even dive—not too deep—into some of your personal life. Commenting on your marital status and the number of kids or perhaps grandkids you have. Maybe you share that you are an only child or the fifteenth of seventeen children in my case. You might wrap up by touching on some of your hobbies and what you enjoy doing outside of work. The intent is to show that you are a well-rounded individual and a good fit for their culture.

But if you were asking yourself the question, or it was not a work situation, you would go farther. As you became comfortable with the individual asking the question, you would affirm your religious affiliation. And if you had no religious attachment, you would share that fact instead. It is part of your identity. And depending on the strength of your convictions, it is a very big part. Woven into the fabric of who you are.

In a study—*The Development of Reasoning about Beliefs: Fact, Preference, and Ideology*—published by the US National Library of Medicine-National Institutes of Health, the authors state that

> religion's influence begins early in development. Five-year-old children categorize individuals based on religious cues (Diesendruck & HaLevi, 2006), and children in elementary school apply theistic reasoning to explanations concerning the natural world (Kelemen, 2004) and the afterlife (Bering, Blasi, & Bjorklund, 2005). Children of this age also demonstrate group-based preferences based on religion (Heiphetz, Spelke, & Banaji, in press), appeal to religion to explain morality (Nucci & Turiel, 1993), and use religious ideas to help them understand themselves, their families, and other people (Coles, 1991). The current research investigates whether children, as well as adults, also differentiate religious beliefs from other types of mental states.[1]

The study goes on to conclude

> that children as young as 5 years of age can systematically judge religious beliefs differently from both fact- and preference-based beliefs. Even 5–6-year-olds make this differentiation, and it continues into adulthood in the same form, suggesting that children and adults have similar conceptions of religious beliefs vis-à-vis other types of beliefs. The fact that adult-like representations of beliefs are present in children suggests that adults do not require many years of experience to arrive at their judgments of conflicting beliefs. Rather, adults' distinction of ideological beliefs from both

---

1. Heiphetz, et al., "Development of Reasoning."

Chapter 8: Forging Ability

factual and preference-based beliefs appears to be the outcome of an early developmental process, and the ability to differentiate a variety of beliefs appears to be an early-emerging component of social cognition.[2]

Our religious beliefs—like all other beliefs—are reinforced and further ingrained by the decisions we make and actions we take throughout our lives. We make friends with people who think like we do because we share similar interests. We join groups and associations of like-minded people. So, we have shared experiences. We interpret data the same and seek knowledge to better understand our world and the world beyond. And in time, we conclude that our beliefs—especially regarding religious matters—are indeed facts and bona fide truths. "Proven" by the community of believers surrounding us. By the time we are adults, these beliefs have been grafted into our DNA. They are as much a part of us as the half-moon birthmark on our left shoulder. To remove, replace, or change them would take time. Lots of time. As well as the hand and scalpel of the most skilled surgeon.

So, why do we turn our beliefs and opinions into knowledge and facts? The short answer. To protect ourselves. It is a defense mechanism. Research, supported by our own personal experience, confirms that human beings fear the unknown. Uncertainty not only scares us but can affect—or some would say distort—how our brains function.

> Scientists[,] including [Ema] Tanovic [who received her PhD in clinical psychology from Yale University, and is currently a principal with the Boston Consulting Group in Philadelphia,] are now making huge strides in explaining why uncertainty can be so excruciating, and delineating the knock-on consequences for our decision-making and behaviour. . . .
>
> In study after study, the researchers found that any element of unpredictability significantly increases people's discomfort, despite there being no objective difference in the intensity of the shock. Participants show greater stress if there is a 50% chance that they might receive a shock, for example, compared to situations in which there is a 100% certainty that they will be electrocuted.
>
> "If we think in purely rational terms, this does not make sense: a 50% chance of a shock should be half as anxiety provoking as a 100% chance if all we care about is the threat itself," says Tanovic. "But this is not how our minds work." . . .

2. Heiphetz, et al., "Development of Reasoning."

> Neuroscientists have started to track the brain activity behind this kind of flawed decision making. The research is still ongoing, but the results so far offer some hints of the neural response to uncertainty. There appears to be heightened activity in the amygdala, for example, which may reflect a state of "hypervigilance," so that we are extra alert to potential risks. Uncertainty also seems to trigger the anterior insula, which is involved in weighing up the consequences of a particular event, and which may inflate the brain's estimates of the potential damage. . . .
>
> In his opinion [Nicholas Carleton, a clinical psychology professor at the University of Regina and scientific director for the Canadian Institute for Public Safety Research and Treatment], the "unknown" represents one of humanity's "fundamental fears"—perhaps even more important to our behaviour than our fear of death.[3]

In a radio interview during the launch of *Gambling With Your Soul*, I was asked, Should we fear death? That's certainly an interesting question. But I think a better or more relevant question is, Why do we fear death? All evidence I've gathered confirms that humans—at least the overwhelming majority—do fear death. And for those that claim not to fear death, when asked why they don't fear death, their answer is most often, "I don't fear death because I know what's going to happen to me when I die." Well, we know that's not true.

Now combine our fundamental fear of the unknown with the specific fear of death. And to be precise, it is the fear of what may come after death. What do we get? We get the perfect storm. In psychological terms, it has been captured in what is called terror management theory. It stems from our unique human condition. The desire, or instinct, as some people have labeled it, for self-preservation coupled with the awareness of certain physical death.

> Terror management theory (TMT) is both a social and evolutionary psychology theory originally proposed by Jeff Greenberg, Sheldon Solomon, and Tom Pyszczynski and codified in their book *The Worm at the Core: On the Role of Death in Life* (2015). It proposes that a basic psychological conflict results from having a self-preservation instinct while realizing that death is inevitable and to some extent unpredictable. This conflict produces terror, which is managed through a combination of escapism and cultural

---

3. Robson, "Why We're So Terrified."

Chapter 8: Forging Ability

beliefs that act to counter biological reality with more significant and enduring forms of meaning and value.

The most obvious examples of cultural values that assuage death anxiety are those that purport to offer literal immortality (e.g., belief in afterlife, religion). However, TMT also argues that other cultural values—including those that are seemingly unrelated to death—offer symbolic immortality. For example, values of national identity, posterity, cultural perspectives on sex, and human superiority over animals have been linked to calm death concerns. In many cases these values are thought to offer symbolic immortality, by either a) providing the sense that one is part of something greater that will ultimately outlive the individual (e.g., country, lineage, species), or b) making one's symbolic identity superior to biological nature (i.e., you are a personality, which makes you more than a glob of cells). Because cultural values influence what is meaningful, they are foundational for self-esteem. TMT describes self-esteem as being the personal, subjective measure of how well an individual is living up to their cultural values.

Terror management theory was developed by social psychologists Greenberg, Solomon, and Pyszczynski. However, the idea of TMT originated from anthropologist Ernest Becker's 1973 Pulitzer Prize-winning work of nonfiction *The Denial of Death*. Becker argues most human action is taken to ignore or avoid the inevitability of death. The terror of absolute annihilation creates such a profound—albeit subconscious—anxiety in people that they spend their lives attempting to make sense of it. On large scales, societies build symbols: laws, religious meaning systems, cultures, and belief systems to explain the significance of life, define what makes certain characteristics, skills, and talents extraordinary, reward others whom they find exemplify certain attributes, and punish or kill others who do not adhere to their cultural worldview. Adherence to these created "symbols" aids in relieving stresses associated with the reality of mortality. On an individual level, self-esteem provides a buffer against death-related anxiety.[4]

To the brain, this is arguably one of the most frightening situations we will ever face. And it is nearly impossible to function with The Question running through our conscious mind. So, most of us push it into our subconscious. Out of sight. Out of mind. However, it does not go away. And when we encounter "life"—someone close to us dies, a story about death in the media catches our attention, we get pulled into a deep

---

4. Wikipedia, "Terror Management Theory."

conversation—The Question is thrust squarely back into our consciousness. Bringing with it the inescapable terror and anxiety. All our natural fear responses kick into high gear.

> The emotion of fear is a core part of human experience. Our brains are wired to experience fear as a way to warn us that we might be in danger....
>
> The human experience of fear begins in the amygdala, the part of the brain that processes many of our emotions. When the amygdala is activated due to possible danger, it elicits the fear response. This can happen when we are in actual danger, when we believe we are in danger, when we experience "scary" stimuli (like a horror movie, for example), or when the amygdala is artificially stimulated.
>
> While the amygdala processes emotional experiences, the frontal lobe and prefrontal cortex control things like language and impulse control. When we experience fear, our brain re-routes energy to the amygdala, slowing down processing in other areas. That is why it can be difficult to speak or make rational decisions when we are afraid.[5]

There are four commonly identified fear responses.

> Fight, flight or freeze are the three most basic stress responses. They reflect how your body will react to danger. Fawn is the fourth stress response that was identified later....
>
> Fight. When your body feels that it is in danger and believes you can overpower the threat, you'll respond in fight mode. Your brain releases signals to your body, preparing it for the physical demands of fighting....
>
> Flight. If your body believes you cannot overcome the danger but can avoid it by running away, you'll respond in flight mode....
>
> Freeze. This stress response causes you to feel stuck in place. This response happens when your body doesn't think you can fight or flight....
>
> Fawn. This response is used after an unsuccessful fight, flight, or freeze attempt.... The fawn response is your body's emotional reaction that involves becoming highly agreeable to the person abusing you.[6]

---

5. Marschall, "Four Fear Responses."
6. Taylor and Bhandari, "Fight, Flight, Freeze, Fawn."

Chapter 8: Forging Ability

When we are afraid, our brain chooses which fear response to use very quickly—almost automatically. Typically, we don't have time to weigh the options and find the best or most appropriate response. But are we able to change our fear response? And if so, how?

> Mindfulness of our emotions can help us to notice when we are having a fear response and try to re-activate the logical part of our brain. When we notice that we are experiencing this response, we can try and make a different choice. Research shows we can train ourselves to respond differently to fear.[7]

Applied to our specific situation of trying to answer The Question—What will happen to me when I die?—our fear responses are inappropriate and ineffective. Let's consider what each fear response would have us do. We start with fight.

In this scenario, since there is not a physical danger, we fight verbally. By arguing that we are right. In other words, defending our current belief. For all the reasons discussed above, we have told ourselves that our belief is the truth. And have turned it into a fact rather than an opinion. And we must turn it into a fact because we understand that to overcome fear, we must make the unknown known. To make something known, we begin by gaining knowledge. And truth is the foundation of knowledge. So, to achieve the knowledge required to answer The Question, we accept our belief as truth. However, deep down we know that we cannot really claim it as truth. We know that no one knows the future. And since our death is a future event, no one knows what will happen to us after we die. So here lies our dilemma with staying and fighting. Raising our voices. Stomping our feet. Pounding our fists. Rolling our eyes. These are all futile attempts to win over our adversary. But, if we are being honest, it is an attempt to win over ourselves. To convince ourselves that we are right. So, we end up getting into an emotionally charged circular argument. One without objective, verifiable evidence, and no one can win it. Therefore, the fight response is not an appropriate response.

The next response is to take flight, flee from danger. Simply run away. In a situation that presents a physical threat, this can be the best response to keep us safe. However, in this specific instance, this response would take the form of not engaging with The Question. Said another way, we would try to get away from The Question—just ignore it. Push it back down into

---

7. Marschall, "Four Fear Responses."

our subconscious. No discussion on or consideration of the topic. In the hope that it will simply go away. Unfortunately, this is not an option. With the simple event of being born, The Question is thrust upon us. And it will remain until we close our eyes for the last time. It will not go away, and we cannot outrun it or hide from it. Even if no one ever verbally asks us The Question, it is still present in our minds. Be it consciously or subconsciously. Hence, the flight response is not an effective response.

We now consider the freeze response. Sometimes, fear can be so overwhelming that it paralyzes us. We take no action. Do nothing. The brain's hope is that the danger will pass us by on its own accord. Leaving us safe and sound in its wake. For our situation of what comes after death, this response is basically the same as the flight response. We try to ignore it, hoping it will go away. As stated above, that is not an option. It will not go away. So, like the flight response, the freeze response is also ineffective.

Lastly, we turn to the fawn response. Our behavior in this response is to try and please whoever is causing the fear. In the situation at hand, the fear is a result of our impending death and the uncertainty associated with what comes next. So, there is no one we can point to as the source of the fear. It is simply the result of our human condition and the knowledge that we will cease to exist in our current physical form. Therefore, the fawn response is not applicable.

We conclude that none of the brain's natural responses to fear are appropriate or effective in addressing The Question. So, how should we respond to this terrifying situation?

We start by returning to habit number two from Stephen R. Covey's *The 7 Habits of Highly Effective People*. "Begin with the End in mind."[8] What "End" do human beings desire? And not just you and I, but all humans? From the first—regardless of how he/she came into being—to the last—regardless of when or how that might occur?

According to some of the world's foremost twenty-first-century philosophers, psychologists, psychoanalysts, and psychotherapists—including Norman Oliver Brown, John Passmore, Kenneth Bancroft Clark, Philip Rieff, Alan Charles Harrington, and Robert Jay Lifton, as well as historical giants like Immanuel Kant, Søren Aabye Kierkegaard, William James, Sigmund Freud, Otto Rank, Carl Gustav Jung, Erich Seligmann Fromm, and many others, every human being, with every fiber of their being, thirsts for immortality. And we seek it in a variety of ways. In fact, some religions were

---

8. Covey, *7 Habits*, 95.

CHAPTER 8: FORGING ABILITY

founded on that premise. They promised that human beings could attain physical immortality. One only had to find the secret, which was reserved for the followers of that specific religion. To date, no one has found the secret.

TMT argues that cultural values can offer us symbolic immortality. Surrogates include national identity, posterity, cultural perspectives on sex, and human superiority over animals. And these things may provide some degree of satisfaction. However, they do not address our true desire for personal, individual immortality.

Other approaches employ philosophical constructs. Some of these may border on the fringes of wishful thinking. Or shall I dare say crosses over into the realm of science fiction. They invoke fantasies of a New Being. Suggesting that mankind will somehow evolve into a new creature that attains the attribute of physical immortality. While maybe a bit far-fetched, it does demonstrate mankind's undeniable hunger to stay in existence. And the lengths we will go to achieve it are endless.

Indeed, some individuals and organizations have gone to great lengths to explore ways of preserving and one day bringing a person back to this physical world after their death—if not preventing death altogether. Ideas differ on how this might be achieved. There are four prevailing approaches:

1. The physical body is restored with the person's soul/mind/consciousness intact. This is the hope of those using cryonics to preserve their bodies. With the rate of advancements in science and technology, extropians are optimistic this practice will someday—in the not-too-distant future—bear fruit. However, thus far, no body that has been mummified or preserved through cryonics has ever been brought back to life.[9]

2. The person's soul/mind/consciousness is captured—referred to as mind uploading or whole brain emulation (WBE)—and transferred into a cyborg—a being with both organic and biomechatronic body parts. This is the approach of the nonprofit organization, the 2045 Initiative, founded by billionaire Russian entrepreneur Dmitry Itskov. "The main goal of the 2045 Initiative, as stated on its website, is 'to create technologies enabling the transfer of an individual's personality to a more advanced non-biological carrier, and extending life, including to the point of immortality. We devote particular attention to enabling

---

9. *Oxford Languages*, "Cryonics."

the fullest possible dialogue between the world's major spiritual traditions, science and society."[10]

3. The person's soul/mind/consciousness is captured and downloaded into a computer where it achieves a kind of digital immortality. "Living" forever in a virtual reality. This path aligns with the idea of a technological singularity, where the intelligence of supercomputers surpasses all human intelligence.[11]

4. Through advances in science and technology—specifically biomedical—a person would never die. Transhumanists advocate for the transformation of a human being into what's called a post-human being—with enhanced abilities that extend a person's life indefinitely.[12]

Now, to be fair, all or some of these four approaches as well as mankind's evolution into a New Being may one day become a reality. But that is a very big may. And if it does become a reality, how far into the future might that be? Well, that is a matter of opinion. But if you are reading or listening to this book, it is safe to assume it will not occur in your lifetime. So, you are still left with The Question and the anxiety that comes with it.

In *The Denial of Death*, Ernest Becker clearly points out "The Limits of Psychotherapy" and "The Limits of Human Nature." He confirms that human beings cannot achieve this fundamental, instinct-driven desire or need by themselves. We must get beyond ourselves. Or said another way, we must get outside of ourselves.[13]

Late in his life, Maslow reached a similar conclusion with his level six (self-transcendence) of human needs. Unfortunately, Maslow's untimely death prevented him from maturing the concept. Nevertheless, his work was continued by several psychologists, including Viktor Emil Frankl, Pamela G. Reed, Claude Robert Cloninger, and Lars Folke Tornstam.[14] They expanded upon and reinforced Maslow's findings. Albeit in slightly different terms and constructs, they all assert that to fully develop as an individual, we must transcend ourselves. Become a part of something larger or greater than ourselves. According to Cloninger, this "may be described as

---

10. Wikipedia, "2045 Initiative."
11. Wikipedia, "Technological Singularity."
12. Wikipedia, "Transhumanism."
13. Becker, *Denial of Death*, 255–285.
14. Wikipedia, "Self-Transcendence."

Chapter 8: Forging Ability

acceptance, identification, or spiritual union with nature and its source."[15] Without this connection, we are incomplete as a human being.

Only an external entity, source, force, nature, the universe, God (whatever name you give it) can fill this need for the individual. Of course, there are many things we can cling to. However, experts have determined that religious immortality ideologies offer the only real solution. And within the religious traditions, those theologies that promote the continuation of the individual (soul, spirit, mind, consciousness, energy, force, etc.—whatever you call that part of a human being which survives physical death) are the most effective in addressing the terror associated with The Question.

While we desire the connectedness with something beyond ourselves, we still want to retain ourselves. Connectedness is what makes us whole. Complete. Yet, we don't want to be a part of an all-encompassing spirit, energy, or God if we lose our individual identity. We would view this as us ceasing to exist. Eliminating the very things that make us "us." Thoughts. Feelings. Sensations. Emotions. Experiences. Memories. In fact, psychologists contend that many conditions identified as mental illnesses—including depression, perversion, and schizophrenia—manifest from our inability to cope with this fundamental psychological conflict. The desire for self-preservation and the knowledge of certain death. Add to this the thought of complete annihilation and the mind cracks.

Over the past hundreds, and maybe thousands, of years through careful study, analysis, experimentation, and observation, the world's most brilliant minds have concluded that this is not what mankind truly desires. We want the individual, self-identified entity of us to exist continuously. Without end. How the desire got inside of us is not something we can or even need to answer. We only need to accept that it is there. It is not something we imagined. It is a bona fide fact. It is the truth.

Based on the analysis in the last chapter—regardless of your belief or the body's natural defense mechanisms, a professional gambler will tell you to always play the odds. Yes, a long shot pays off once in a blue moon. But to put food on the table consistently, the odds are the way to go.

To assess the long-term viability of a project, a foundational class on business principles or project management would introduce you to the subject of risk management. It employs the sage maxim of hope for the best but plan for the worst. In the afterlife possibilities identified, spending a tormented eternity in hell/the lake of fire—advocated by Christianity,

---

15. Wikipedia, "Self-Transcendence."

Islam, some adherents of African traditional and diasporic religions, and Judaism—is the worst possible outcome. You should plan, and with this specific project, "plan" equates to *live your life* in such a manner to avoid this outcome.

And a Stoic will tell you that Christianity is the appropriate reasoned choice.

But our choices are not always reasonable, logical, or rational. Aside from the brain's programmed responses to fear, our choices are derived from our beliefs. And we often form a belief—or said another way, an opinion—based on how we feel. Or what someone else tells us—whether they can prove it or not. And the person's words carry significant weight if it is someone we know, trust, respect, admire, is famous, powerful, smart, etc. Or any other number of factors.

At this precise moment in time, we are a composition of every thought, word, action, and experience we have ever had. Each of these has been influenced significantly by our surroundings. We are a product of our environment. And one of the largest determinants of our environment are the people with whom we interact. They have a tremendous impact on us. From the way we talk to the way we walk. From the games we play to the places we stay. From what we drink to what we think. Either negatively or positively. And it begins in each of our households, or its equivalent, from birth.

Long before we start to make any cognitive decisions for ourselves, our parents, siblings, and those closest to us are forming us. Laying the foundation and building upon it with their words and actions—a by-product of their own beliefs. "Psychologists believe that by the age of seven, most of our patterns of behaviour, our beliefs and our habits are formed."[16] And following the footsteps of those closest to us may be the best approach to address many topics. But is it the best way to approach this topic? The afterlife. And more specifically, our own afterlife—The Question to which no one has the answer.

Gambling With Your Soul: What Is Your Best Bet? proved that Christianity is your best bet. But how do you make Christianity your reasoned choice? We have already determined that left to its natural behavior, in response to the fear invoked by The Question, the brain will not lead us to a logical decision. In fact, it will cause us to make an irrational and illogical decision. To help put us on the right path—a logical decision tree if you

---

16. Fox, "Age of 7."

Chapter 8: Forging Ability

will—let's revisit the fate of an atheist compared to that of a Christian in the last chapter.

Many atheists did not begin life as an atheist. They were first steeped in the prevailing religion of the geographical region in which they were born—Christianity, Islam, Hinduism, Buddhism, etc. Then, at some point in their lives, they stopped believing in that religion. Reasons vary from individual to individual. Most often it revolves around a lack of proof to confirm the religion is "right" in what it teaches.

This inability to provide the requested proof goes far beyond questions regarding the afterlife. And it often boils down to proving God's existence. But we will set that aside for our discussion and focus only on the request for proof of an afterlife. And not just any afterlife, but the specific one being promoted by the religion to confirm it is the truth. And to make the point more exact, the proof would need to be given to the individual asking the question at this precise moment in time—and not some arbitrary person or historical figure. We want proof that we will have the afterlife the religion is promising. So, in the case of Christianity, proof that there is a heaven and a hell. Both locations are eternal. And furthermore, that we will go to heaven if we put our faith in Jesus Christ.

When put into an investment or business scenario, the demand for proof of a future event would be considered ridiculous. Let's say you want to buy a stock. When deciding what stock to purchase, would you demand proof that the stock will be at a certain price seven years in the future? And if you did make such a demand, would there be a financial advisor brazen enough to provide an answer? And if there was a less than scrupulous advisor who did provide a price, equating to a guarantee, would you buy it? Of course not. You know that no individual knows the future.

A fortune teller's crystal ball reading comes with statements like, "If you do such and such, or don't do such and such, then this is what I see." It has long been a standard disclaimer in the financial investment community to indicate that, "Past results are not a guarantee of future results." After singing the praises of any new drug, a professional speed reader makes us aware of all the potential side effects at a thousand words a minute. While we can't understand a word he is saying, we get the message. This drug may not work for you. Or worse. It may be fatal. And when asking about the weather, even Alexa will tell you, "Here's the forecast for tomorrow in Chandler. Look for lots of sun, with a high of ninety-nine and a low of seventy-seven degrees." She knows that you will not know Chandler's weather for tomorrow until you get to tomorrow.

That is the same for what comes after death. We will not know the truth of our afterlife until we get to our afterlife—and stay there. But we still want a forecast. And, along with scientific research noted above, Anthony "Tony" Robbins says we must have one. It addresses one of the six core needs that we have as human beings. In his book *The Driving Force: The Six Human Needs*, the first need identified is certainty—the need for safety, stability, security, comfort, order, predictability, control, and consistency. This reduces our inherent fear of the unknown.[17]

So, what is the best way to make a choice regarding an uncertain future event? We make an informed decision by following an objective and disciplined decision-making process. Research, experience, and real-world events confirm that human beings make better decisions when using a structured decision-making process, keeping emotions—as much as possible—out of the equation. A Google search yields numerous examples, with anywhere from four to nine steps. Regardless of the number of steps, they all include a step—usually the final one—to evaluate the outcome or results of the decision. This is especially meaningful for our situation regarding The Question. We will come back to this later. Below is the process put forth by the University of Massachusetts in Dartmouth:

Step 1: Identify the decision
You realize that you need to make a decision. Try to clearly define the nature of the decision you must make. This first step is very important.

Step 2: Gather relevant information
Collect some pertinent information before you make your decision: what information is needed, the best sources of information, and how to get it. This step involves both internal and external "work." Some information is internal: you'll seek it through a process of self-assessment. Other information is external: you'll find it online, in books, from other people, and from other sources.

Step 3: Identify the alternatives
As you collect information, you will probably identify several possible paths of action, or alternatives. You can also use your imagination and additional information to construct new alternatives. In this step, you will list all possible and desirable alternatives.

17. Robbins, *Personal Power*, 1.

Chapter 8: Forging Ability

Step 4: Weigh the evidence
Draw on your information and emotions to imagine what it would be like if you carried out each of the alternatives to the end. Evaluate whether the need identified in Step 1 would be met or resolved through the use of each alternative. As you go through this difficult internal process, you'll begin to favor certain alternatives: those that seem to have a higher potential for reaching your goal. Finally, place the alternatives in a priority order, based upon your own value system.

Step 5: Choose among the alternatives
Once you have weighed all the evidence, you are ready to select the alternative that seems to be [the] best one for you. You may even choose a combination of alternatives. Your choice in Step 5 may very likely be the same or similar to the alternative you placed at the top of your list at the end of Step 4.

Step 6: Take action
You're now ready to take some positive action by beginning to implement the alternative you chose in Step 5.

Step 7: Review your decision and its consequences
In this final step, consider the results of your decision and evaluate whether or not it has resolved the need you identified in Step 1. If the decision has *not* met the identified need, you may want to repeat certain steps of the process or make a new decision. For example, you might want to gather more detailed or somewhat different information or explore additional alternatives.[18]

If you have reached this point in the book, or have read *Gambling With Your Soul*, you will recognize this as the process we have followed. It brought us to our conclusion that Christianity is the best bet. We have completed Step 5 and are on the threshold of launching into Step 6. Now comes the hard part. The real work. What if the best alternative does not align with our current belief or opinion? What if it is not the answer we were hoping for? What do we do? We ask for more data. More time. We start to second guess the analysis. These are the telltale signs of what is known as analysis paralyses. It is another form of the freeze response to fear. Our fear of The Question. Our fear of change, which in psychology is known as metathesiophobia. It is a persistent, abnormal, and unwarranted phobia that causes

---
18. UMass Dartmouth, "Decision-Making Process."

people to avoid changing their circumstances due to being extremely afraid of the unknown.[19] We must fight against this tendency. Push forward. Act.

But, even when this proven decision-making process tells us that Christianity is the right decision, we cannot flip a switch and make ourselves adopt a new belief. The new belief could be one hundred and eighty degrees from our current belief. Some beliefs involve more than the mind. They pull on the heart and are felt in our bones. We may have had experiences which cemented our belief into our psyche. So, how do we change? Can we change?

As indicated earlier in the article "The Four Fear Responses: Fight, Flight, Freeze, and Fawn," research does confirm our ability to change. We can train our brains to respond differently from its natural reflexes. And like all change, it starts with an awareness of the need for change. If we are not a Christian, and the Christian afterlife turns out to be correct, we start by accepting that we cannot achieve our desire—to avoid a bad afterlife—with our current belief. We also acknowledge that The Question evokes fear in us. With an understanding of our brain's natural responses to fear, we admit that those responses are inappropriate and ineffective. They will lead us to make an emotional and irrational decision, which will not be the best choice. And therefore, not in our best interest. So, we move forward with deliberate action.

We must create new experiences. Gather new data points. Experts today tell us that on average it takes sixty-six days for a person to form a new habit. But depending on the person and the habit, it could range from eighteen to two hundred and fifty-four days.[20] In complete alignment with modern-day science, very similar advice was given hundreds of years ago. To help non-Christians with this dilemma in the seventeenth century, Blaise Pascal had this to say:

> But at least learn your inability to believe, since reason brings you to this, and yet you cannot believe. Endeavour then to convince yourself, not by increase of proofs of God, but by the abatement of your passions. You would like to attain faith, and do not know the way; you would like to cure yourself of unbelief and ask the remedy for it. Learn of those who have been bound like you, and who now stake all their possessions. These are people who know the way which you would follow, and who are cured of an ill of

---

19. Wiktionary, "Metathesiophobia."
20. Wikipedia, "Habit."

Chapter 8: Forging Ability

which you would be cured. Follow the way by which they began; by acting as if they believed, taking the holy water, having masses said, etc. Even this will naturally make you believe, and deaden your acuteness.[21]

According to Wikipedia, "Old habits are hard to break and new habits are hard to form because the behavioural patterns which humans repeat become imprinted in neural pathways, but it is possible to form new habits through repetition."[22] In addition to the scientific approach of repetition, or Pascal's "fake it 'til you make it" remedy, as human beings, we have been gifted with the ability to imagine. Our imagination—recall the advice in step four of the decision-making process—allows us to form an opinion, hold a belief, and develop a steadfast conviction about something even if we are not able to prove it as being the truth. When deciding whether to become a Christian, I encourage you—like many world-class athletes who frequently rely on visualization to help them win major sports competitions—to use this most incredible and powerful ability. And all other methods, strategies, or techniques available to you. The odds are too low, the stakes are too high, and the consequences are too severe if you are wrong.

If we could be right with every decision, or at least the major ones, that would be awesome. It would be a significant enabler to fulfill the self-esteem need identified at level four of Maslow's hierarchy. And according to Maslow, it may be a bona fide requirement. Maslow further asserts that we must fulfill the needs at this level to have an opportunity to reach our full potential—every person's desire. And that happens through self-actualization and self-transcendence found at levels five and six.

With most actions, the outcome from our decision is realized within our lifetime. This could be immediately or within a few hours, days, weeks, or months. As instructed in step seven, we can use the knowledge gained from the actual outcome to help with future decisions. Where we are wrong, we would learn from our mistakes and make an adjustment in our decision-making process. Allowing us to avoid another undesired result. Where we are right, we would have confirmation that our decision-making process is sound and continue deploying it on future decisions.

In the context of the afterlife, our task is especially daunting since we do not have the benefit of assessing the outcome of previous decisions in this area. We certainly cannot evaluate our own personal decision since

---

21. Pascal, quoted in Wikipedia, "Pascal's Wager."
22. Wikipedia, "Habit."

we have not died and come back to life. Now here, we are not referring to a near-death experience (NDE) or someone who was in a coma, no matter the length of time, then regained consciousness. We would need to have been dead for a significant amount of time—say at least three months—then came back to life. And we also cannot turn to the decisions of others for guidance.

Do we know the whereabouts of our departed loved ones? What about the individual—or more precisely, the individual's soul—who started or inspired the formation of the religion/nonreligion we have chosen to follow? Our first instinct is to answer affirmatively. Yes. Of course, I know. As human beings, we fear the unknown. To reduce that fear, we convince ourselves that we do know. However, based on our understanding of the word *know*, that is regrettably not the truth. And that goes against everything we have been taught and most likely contradicts what we have told others. That is incredibly difficult and unsettling for us to even think about, much less accept. It evokes thoughts, feelings, and sensations that are truly terrifying. And that makes this decision different from most—if not all—other situations we face during our lifetime. We cannot complete the decision-making process, which adds to an already anxiety-producing predicament. Nonetheless, we must decide. And in fact, we have already made the decision—either willingly or unwillingly.

I recently listened to a debate presented by the Veritas Forum as one of the Best of 2022 Podcasts. When I tuned in, it was entitled "Living Well in Light of Death." However, when it was originally recorded at Yale—in 2014—it was called "Living Well in the Light of Death." The program featured N. T. Wright, a bible scholar and former bishop. His sparring partner was Shelly Kagan, a professor of philosophy. Late in the podcast, Wright posed a question to Kagan regarding his confidence in materialism—an underlying philosophy of atheism—being true. Kagan responded by admitting that he would not stake his life on it being true. He said, "If God were to come down now and say, you know, Are you prepared to bet whether or not materialism is true? I'll give you a hundred bucks if you're right and I'll kill you if you're wrong. I'm not taking that bet."

Unfortunately, for Professor Kagan and all of us, we are not afforded the opportunity to decide if we want to take that bet. With the simple event of being born, the bet is thrust upon us. For each of us, the reality of physical mortality demands that we lay our life on the line. Betting that our belief is true. Is that fair? Maybe not, but it is the hand we are dealt. And it makes

Chapter 8: Forging Ability

no difference how we got here. Whether from the big bang, with its origins tied to quantum uncertainty, then evolving through natural selection. Or from Adam and Eve, who were formed out of dust by God, then told to be fruitful and multiply. We cannot undo what has been done to get us here.

Now certainly there is some value in understanding one's past. But its usefulness has limitations. Looking only in the rear-view mirror to navigate the winding road ahead of us will land us in the ditch. We also can't hand off the responsibility to someone else. And claiming to have no belief regarding the afterlife—attempting to ignore the bet—is likewise not an option. In some religious traditions, having no belief is—for all intents and purposes—the same as saying there is no afterlife or no God. Therefore, since our only option is to take the bet, we choose the alternative that gives us the best chance to be a winner—regardless of which afterlife possibility turns out to be the truth.

Reflections

What movies, books, people, events, or experiences have shaped your beliefs about the afterlife?

_____
_____
_____
_____
_____
_____

How do you envision eternity?

_____
_____
_____
_____
_____
_____

How do you feed your soul?

_____
_____
_____
_____
_____
_____

Conclusion

> The world and its desires pass away,
> but whoever does the will of God lives forever.
>
> —1 John 2:17 (NIV)

WE LEARNED IN PART I that to win with our bodies, we must put in the work. Eat a healthy diet. Get enough sleep. Exercise and train the right way for the right amount of time—days, months, or years depending on the skill needed to achieve our goal. And that the training is both physical and mental. We learned about the power of the mind to control the body and the indisputable benefit of visualization. We were reminded that the body cannot achieve what the mind cannot conceive. And finally, we saw what it takes to build muscle, muscle memory, endurance, strength, and flexibility. We acknowledged the inescapable demand imposed by the laws of physics to push the body beyond its current limits. Fight through the pain. These are the ingredients for the body to achieve peak performance.

In part II, we learned that to win with our minds we must train the mind. Whether it's one with the brain—as advocated by monists—or a separate entity/substance—as advocated by dualists, the mind requires conditioning just like the body. We must create a daily routine to tune it. Focus it. Block out all distractions at times. And most importantly, develop a positive, growth mindset—stretching the mind and expanding our perspective. Or as David Asomaning would say in *Nightmares to Miracles*, we need to adopt a "miracle mindset," allowing us to turn nightmares into miracles.[1] See the glass half full instead of half empty. Have an expectation that every problem has a solution. View every experience, regardless of the outcome, as a learning opportunity. A chance to gain more knowledge, which leads to

---

1. Asomaning, *Nightmares to Miracles*, 126.

Winning with Your Body, Mind, and Soul

wisdom and understanding. Develop a mental toughness. Build grit. They say, "What doesn't kill you, makes you stronger." Well, it does with the right mindset.

And lastly, in part III, we learned what it takes to win with our souls. We embraced the necessity to free ourselves, our souls, through the healing power of forgiveness. Having concluded in *Gambling With Your Soul* that Christianity is our best bet, we learned how one might go about becoming a Christian. We accepted our fear of uncertainty and death. Then gained insight into our brain's natural responses to fear. We came to realize that—left to its normal course of reaction—the brain will lead us to make an irrational decision when addressing The Question: What will happen to me when I die? And thankfully, we can overcome this evolutionary response by using a structured decision-making process—minimizing the amygdala's influence and keeping our emotions in check.

As discussed in the introduction, we want to reach our full potential. To be all that we can be. Become self-fulfilled/self-actualized and then reach the pinnacle of human development with self-transcendence. And to do that, we must win with the body, mind, and soul. Separately and collectively.

You have probably heard the expression, "It's lonely at the top." I believe this applies to all winners, who are at the top of their game for the endeavor in which they are engaged. Regardless of a person's professional or personal pursuits—acting, business, cooking, dancing, education, painting, parenting, politics, public speaking, religion, science, singing, sports, etc.—to win, they must spend time marrying their desire and ability to come out on top. And much of the work to get there is solitary. Alone time. We must get away from the crowds. Away from the hustle and bustle. Take a break from the rat race. Away from our everyday life—spouse, kids, parents, siblings, friends, coworkers, teammates, television, the radio, the internet. Unplugged.

My executive coach once said to me, "Henry, you care too much about what other people think." At first, this was quite confusing. Because in another breath, he talked about the importance of building emotional intelligence. Being a caring, compassionate, and empathetic leader. So, how do you do that if you do not care what other people think?

As our sessions continued, I came to understand his comment. It is important, very important, to listen and hear what others have to say. Ensure they know you have heard them, taken their input seriously, and given

CONCLUSION

it proper consideration. However, as the leader, you, and you alone, are ultimately responsible for the decision and the consequences of that decision. The good, the bad, and the ugly.

As leaders of our own selves, we are each responsible for the decisions we make and their consequences for our lives. No one can stand in our place. Not at birth, throughout our lives, at death, or beyond. Certainly, we desire to be a winner with each of the three human components—body, mind, and soul. But if we had to pick only one where winning was possible, which one do we choose? Or said another way, for which one is winning the most important? The soul. Why? It is the only one with even the possibility of having a permanent existence. Being everlasting. Or as followers of Tenrikyo or Rastafarianism would say, "everliving." And it is the only one that can satisfy our primal desire for personal immortality.

Let's revisit the record-setting race in part I: "Winning With Your Body." As stated earlier, our desire was to save the men's lightweight freshman rowing program at Yale. That was the war we were fighting. The 1983 EARC Eastern Sprints men's lightweight freshman grand finals was a battle within the war. It was one of many battles in the war, and it was certainly an important and strategic one. Winning it moved us, and the entire effort, closer to winning the war—saving the men's lightweight freshman rowing program. However, the war continued long after our victory.

> In June 2012, the Intercollegiate Rowing Association (IRA) decided to allow freshmen to compete in the IRA National Championship regatta. . . . This decision applied only to the national championship. . . .
> Then, when the Ivy League administrators heard of the change, they voted to open freshman eligibility to all levels of varsity competition throughout the entire spring season. . . .
> "The freshman category worked fine," [lightweight crew coach Andy] Card said in an email to the News. "There was less pressure on each freshman to get to a varsity level right away."[2]

For the 2015 rowing season, Yale officially eliminated the men's lightweight freshman rowing program. So, with our 1983 EARC Eastern Sprints victory, did we win? In a perfect world, we would win every battle and win the war. But we know the world is not perfect. Would you rather win every battle and lose the war? Or lose every battle and win the war?

2. Uniat, "Freshman Rowers."

What battles are you fighting that are part of a larger war? I encourage you to take a break and think—I mean *really* think—about this next question. Do I *want* to die? And not just from a physical perspective. But cease to exist in every way possible. Whatever that means to you. Regardless of what you believe will happen to you. Or what your religion/nonreligion has said will happen to you. What do you *want* to happen? Stop. Put down this book. Eliminate all distractions. Be quiet and be still for at least a few minutes.

###

Okay. Let's resume.

Ecclesiastes 3:11 tells us that "he has made everything beautiful in its time. He has also set eternity in the human heart; yet no one can fathom what God has done from beginning to end" (NIV). And the Amplified Bible further explains that "he has made everything beautiful *and* appropriate in its time. He has also planted eternity [a sense of divine purpose] in the human heart [a mysterious longing which nothing under the sun can satisfy, except God]—yet man cannot find out (comprehend, grasp) what God has done (His overall plan) from the beginning to the end."

Competitions with the body are battles. Competitions with the mind are battles. Competition with the soul is war. The War. As advised by Eph 6:12, "For we are not fighting against flesh-and-blood enemies, but against evil rulers and authorities of the unseen world, against mighty powers in this dark world, and against evil spirits in the heavenly places" (NLT). Winning with the body and the mind are only paper victories. Winning with the soul is the only victory that really matters in The End.

If we are extremely healthy, lucky, blessed—you pick the word—our bodies may last one hundred years. Over time, the effects of gravity and a host of other natural forces take over. Beauty fades. Muscles weaken. Bones soften. Speed diminishes. Organs fail. And the duration of the mind would be equal to or less than the number of days for our physical body. Global statistics reveal that a significant number of humans suffer some form of mental degradation during their lifetime. In the United States, as of February 2022, the Alzheimer's Association reports that "one in three seniors dies with Alzheimer's or another dementia."[3]

---

3. Alzheimer's Association, "Facts and Figures."

CONCLUSION

So, like a laser beam, we focus on securing victory for our soul. According to Rom 10:17, "faith comes from hearing the message, and the message is heard through the word of Christ" (NIV). It is my desire that you have heard Christ's message through these pages. But this book could only serve as a brief introduction to the Christian faith. I urge you to find a Christian community to connect with. It could be as small as one or two individuals. As soon as possible, fulfill the two foundational acts described in Rom 10:9, which states "that if you confess with your mouth, 'Jesus is Lord,' and believe in your heart that God raised him from the dead, you will be saved" (NIV). Keep in mind that having your belief confirmed as the truth is not the requirement. But only that you think it is true, and act in accordance with that belief. Then take the necessary steps to strengthen your new belief—crawl, walk, run.

Do not let anyone tell you that you need to *know* in your heart that God raised Jesus from the dead. I am convinced the word *believe* is intentional. It requires trust. Faith. Letting go of the inherent fear of the unknown buried—perhaps subconsciously—within you. Relinquishing your drive and need for certainty.

The world attaches a negative connotation to not knowing something. You are called dumb. Made to feel like you are stupid, ignorant, or gullible. God forbid if you were to admit out loud that you do not know what will happen to yourself when you die. With that admission, even if you met every other requirement to be a Christian, some people would tell you that you are not a Christian. Or at least not a "real" Christian. Imagine telling a baby or an elderly person if they cannot drive a car or change their own diaper, then they are not human beings.

The world will try and tell you that if you do not do a certain thing. Look a certain way. Act a certain way. Think a certain way. Then you are not an XYZ. Or at least not a "real" XYZ. The people doing this may not even be aware of their behavior. It is often done unconsciously to protect themselves from their own fears and insecurities.

"In psychoanalytic theory, a defence mechanism (American English: defense mechanism), is an unconscious psychological operation that functions to protect a person from anxiety-producing thoughts and feelings related to internal conflicts and outer stressors. Defence mechanisms may result in healthy or unhealthy consequences depending on the circumstances and frequency with which the mechanism is used. Defence mechanisms (German: *Abwehrmechanismen*) are psychological strategies brought into play by the unconscious mind to manipulate, deny, or distort reality in order to defend against feelings of anxiety and unacceptable impulses and to maintain one's self-schema or other schemas."[4]

As Philippe advised me on our ride from JFK International Airport to Yale, "Don't buy it." Your relationship with God, which encompasses your belief in, trust in, and faith in God, is between you and God. If he, she, or it exists. It's based on what is in your heart. And no human can know that.

Being able to admit that you do not know what will happen to you when you die is smart. Very smart. And takes a tremendous amount of courage and wisdom. It will not only make you a better Christian, but a better person. Proverbs 1:7 tells us that "the fear of the Lord is the beginning of knowledge, but fools despise wisdom and instruction" (NIV). "The Hebrew word translated into 'awe' in the Bible is yirah (יראה, pronounced yir-ah). It often directly translates into fear, but it can also mean respect, reverence, and worship. But make no mistake about it, yirah is strongly connected to 'trembling.'"[5] The famous Christian Serenity Prayer—written by the American theologian Reinhold Niebuhr in 1932–1933—makes the request that "God, grant me the serenity to accept the things I cannot change, courage to change the things I can, and wisdom to know the difference."[6] You cannot change the fact that you do not know what will happen to you when you die… until you die. And stay dead.

So, with that knowledge, you make the best decision possible based on humanity's collective experience. Accumulated over millions of years and trillions of hours. Data that has been gathered under controlled and uncontrolled settings. Some collected from physical entities, and some from nonphysical entities. Accounting for every species known to mankind. And like a coxswain on race day, you turn the mountain of data into something useful. Information. Information to develop and execute a winning strategy for your life. A strategy that accounts for the known present (i.e., the certainty of physical death) and, more importantly, the unknown future (i.e., the potential for life after death).

You accept your logical, reasoned, and rational decision—Christianity is the best bet—once and for all and eliminate the fear and anxiety associated with The Question. Jesus said in Matt 11:28, "Come to me, all you who are weary and burdened, and I will give you rest" (NIV). Not only physical

---

4. Wikipedia, "Defence Mechanism."
5. FIRM, "Hebrew Meaning of Yirah."
6. Wikipedia, "Serenity Prayer."

CONCLUSION

rest for your body. Or rest for your mind. But rest for your soul as well. Rest for your whole self—body, mind, and soul. Separately and collectively. Rest from wrestling with The Question.

If you are not a Christian, this is your only way. Make no mistake. There is no other path to the sweet spot. No chance of winning the war. Winning with your soul. And you cannot sit on the fence or straddle the road, choosing not to make a declaration for any specific belief or religion. Jesus took that option away in Matt 12:30 when he declared that "anyone who isn't with me opposes me, and anyone who isn't working with me is actually working against me" (NLT).

You can have the voice of an angel or cannot carry a note as far as you can throw an elephant. You may have a face that stops time or one that makes people wonder if you escaped from the zoo. Your IQ can be off the charts or the equivalent of a rock. You can be the most gifted litigator to ever set foot in a courtroom, or you can break out in a cold sweat at the thought of public speaking. You can have jokes that make a crocodile smile or dry enough to put your funny bone to sleep. You may be the best or the worst athlete the world has ever seen. You can be the most skillful surgeon to ever enter an operating room or faint at the sight of blood. You may be able to write a story that takes the reader to another world, or you cannot string two words together to save your life. You may be able to deliver a line that brings the words on a page to life or get tongue-tied in front of a camera. You can be serving in the pulpit or the big house. You can command the most powerful army, corporation, team, etc. in the universe or be at the bottom of the totem pole. You may have more money than God. Or you cannot rub two nickels together.

None of these things will matter if you stand before Jesus Christ after your physical life is over. In *The Denial of Death*, Ernest Becker does a masterful job of summarizing the various approaches—through a psychological lens—mankind employs to cope with our uniquely human condition. Our desire for self-preservation coupled with the awareness of certain physical death. In the book's final section, "The Fusion of Science and Religion," Becker ends with these sobering words:

> The most that any one of us can seem to do is to fashion something—an object or ourselves—and drop it into the confusion, make an offering of it, so to speak, to the life force.[7]

---

7. Becker, *Denial of Death*, 285.

Winning with Your Body, Mind, and Soul

And I submit that the object we should fashion is ourselves—body, mind, and soul—and offer it to Jesus Christ, who is the life force. Or has a direct line to it. We should put our faith in him and take him at his word when he said, in John 14:6, "I am the way and the truth and the life. No one comes to the Father except through me" (NIV).

While this is certainly no laughing matter, allow me to share a joke I recently heard. Satan convened a strategic planning session with his executive team. "As you know, we are in a fierce competition with God and his angels to see who can gather the most souls," Satan began. "It's a very tight race. What are some ideas for us to pull ahead?" The first demon general stood up and said, "I have an idea. Let's convince mankind there is no heaven." "Yeah . . . that'll work!" the other demons shouted. Lucifer thought for a moment, then concluded, "I don't think so. With all the bad things we're causing on Earth, it will be impossible to convince mankind there is not a better place when they die."

The second demon general stood up and said, "I have an idea. Let's convince mankind there is no hell." "Yeah . . . that'll work!" the other demons shouted. Lucifer thought for a moment, then concluded, "I don't think so. Since mankind is convinced there is a good place when they die, it will be illogical to suggest there is not a bad place as well. Mankind is too smart for that. They won't buy it."

The lowest-ranking demon general stood up and said, "I have an idea. Let's convince mankind there is no hurry. They have all the time in the world. They can find Jesus later." Satan shouted, "Aha! That's it!"

Before it's too late, I hope you go all in, taking Anne Wilson's advice, "And let my Jesus change your life."[8]

> Your beliefs become your thoughts,
> Your thoughts become your words,
> Your words become your actions,
> Your actions become your habits,
> Your habits become your values,
> Your values become your destiny.
> —Gandhi

---

8. Anne Wilson et al. "My Jesus," Jacobs Story Music, Capitol CMG, 2021.

CONCLUSION

Reflections

Review your answers in Reflections at the end of parts I, II, and III. Would you change any responses?

_____
_____
_____
_____
_____

Who in your life should read this book?

_____
_____
_____
_____
_____

What are your next steps?

_____
_____
_____
_____
_____

Bibliography

Alzheimer's Association. "Alzheimer's Disease: Facts and Figures." 2024. https://www.alz.org/alzheimers-dementia/facts-figures.
Answers. "What Do Rastafarians Believe about the Afterlife?" Last updated Oct. 2, 2011. http://wiki.answers.com/Q/What_do_rastafarians_believe_about_the_afterlife.
Asomaning, David. *Nightmares to Miracles*. Published by the author, 2022.
Aurin. "The Holocaust and Jack Schwarz." *Six Perfections* (blog). Dec. 28, 2012. http://sixperfections.blogspot.com/2012/12/the-holocaust-and-jack-schwarz.html.
BBC. "Modern Spiritualism: Beliefs." Religions, last updated Sept. 9, 2009. http://www.bbc.co.uk/religion/religions/spiritualism/beliefs/beliefs_1.shtml.
———. "Jainism: The Soul." Religions, last updated Sept. 10, 2009. http://www.bbc.co.uk/religion/religions/jainism/beliefs/soul.shtml.
Becker, Ernest. *The Denial of Death*. New York: Free Press, 1973.
Beliefnet. "What Neo-pagans Believe: Central Tenets of Neo-paganism, Based on the Questions in the Belief-O-Matic Quiz." June 2001. https://www.beliefnet.com/faiths/2001/06/what-neo-pagans-believe.aspx.
The Bhagavad Gita. Translated by Winthrop Sargeant. New York: Excelsior Editions, 2009.
Borek, Tyler. "Oarsmen Must Win to Keep Shirts on Their Backs." *Yale News*, Apr. 9, 2008. https://yaledailynews.com/blog/2008/04/09/oarsmen-must-win-to-keep-shirts-on-their-backs/.
Bullock, Olivia. "What Happens When You Die? A Look at Different Chinese Mythologies on Death and the Afterlife: According to Traditional Chinese Mythology/Folk Religions." https://web.archive.org/web/20180701000000*/https://www.theworldofchinese.com/2014/10/what-happens-when-you-die/.
Camps, Marc Arenas. "How Many Species Live on Earth?" *All You Need Is Biology* (blog). May 20, 2018. https://allyouneedisbiology.wordpress.com/2018/05/20/biodiversity-species/.
Covey, Stephen R. *The 7 Habits of Highly Effective People*. New York: Simon & Schuster, 1989.
Davis, Henry Arnold. *Gambling With Your Soul: What Is Your Best Bet?* Eugene, OR: Resource Publications, 2021.
Dawkins, Richard. *The God Delusion*. New York: Mariner, 2008. First published 2006 by Bantam Press (London).
"Decision-Making Process: 7 Steps to Effective Decision Making." UMass Dartmouth. https://www.umassd.edu/fycm/decision-making/process/.

Bibliography

Denosky, J. "Spiritualism and Spiritual Travel: A Spiritualist's View of After-Death States." *Travel in the Spiritual Worlds.* http://www.spiritualtravel.org/OBE/spiritualist.html.

eCondolence.com. "Understanding Shinto." https://www.econdolence.com/learning-center/religion-and-culture/shinto/understanding-shinto.

Encyclopedia Britannica Online. "Tenrikyō: Japanese Religion." Last updated Oct. 16, 2015. https://www.britannica.com/topic/Tenrikyo.

Fellowship of Israel Related Ministries (FIRM). "Hebrew Meaning of Yirah: What Connects Fear and Awe?" Learning Center, July 20, 2021. https://firmisrael.org/learn/hebrew-meaning-of-yirah-what-connects-fear-and-awe/#:~:text=The%20Hebrew%20word%20translated%20into,strongly%20connected%20to%20'trembling.

FindYourFate.com. "Rastafari." Life after Death. https://death.findyourfate.com/life-after-death/rastafari.html.

Fox, Carol. "By the Age of 7 Most of Our Beliefs and Habits Are Formed." Mar. 7, 2019. https://www.linkedin.com/pulse/age-7-most-our-beliefs-habits-formed-carol-fox.

The Free Dictionary. "Give the Shirt off One's Back, To." Idioms, last updated Aug. 10, 2024. https://idioms.thefreedictionary.com/give+the+shirt+off+your+back.

Gardiner, Eileen. "About Zoroastrian Hell." *Hell-On-Line* (blog). Revised Mar. 2, 2008. http://www.hell-on-line.org/AboutZOR.html.

Good Reads. "René Descartes." Quotable Quote. https://www.goodreads.com/quotes/28930-if-you-would-be-a-real-seeker-after-truth-it.

Got Questions. "Do Jews Believe in Hell?" Last updated Oct. 20, 2023. https://www.gotquestions.org/do-Jews-believe-in-hell.html.

Hafiz, Yasmine. "Yazidi Religious Beliefs: History, Facts and Traditions of Iraq's Persecuted Minority." *HuffPost*, Apr. 13, 2014. Last updated Sept. 6, 2016. https://www.huffpost.com/entry/yazidi-religious-beliefs_n_5671903.

Hathaway, Bill. "Yale Researchers Have a Formula for Getting in the Flow." *Yale News*, Apr. 26, 2022. https://news.yale.edu/2022/04/26/yale-researchers-have-formula-getting-flow?utm_source=YaleToday&utm_medium=Email&utm_campaign=YT_Yale%20Today%20Best%20of%20the%20Week%20Alumni%20no%20Parents_5-7-2022.

Heiphetz, Larisa, et al. "The Development of Reasoning about Beliefs: Fact, Preference, and Ideology." *J Exp Soc Psychol* 49.3 (2013) 559–565. doi:10.1016/j.jesp.2012.09.005.

Hinga, Teresia Mbari. "Afterlife: African Concepts." Encyclopedia.com, 2005. https://www.encyclopedia.com/environment/encyclopedias-almanacs-transcripts-and-maps/afterlife-african-concepts.

Horton, Sarah J. "Shinto." *Encyclopedia of Death and Dying.* http://www.deathreference.com/Sh-Sy/Shinto.html.

Hosseini, Seyedehbehnaz. "Life after Death in Manichaeism and Yārsān." *Fritillaria Kurdica* 13–14 (2016) 3–34. https://www.academia.edu/34751046/Life_after_Death_in_Manichaeism_and_Y%C4%81rs%C4%81n.

Humanists UK. "Non-religious Beliefs." https://humanists.uk/humanism/humanism-today/non-religious-beliefs/.

Khalsa, Sukhmandir. "Sikhism and the Afterlife." Learn Religions, Sept. 2, 2024. http://sikhism.about.com/od/sikhism101/qt/Sikh_Afterlife.htm.

Leggett, Hadley. "Mental Health Hygiene Can Improve Mood, Decrease Stress." Stanford Medicine, May 11, 2022. https://scopeblog.stanford.edu/2022/05/11/mental-health-hygiene-can-improve-mood-decrease-stress/?mkt_tok=ODgoLUZTQiozMDcAAAGElk6adB6-KC6SMw1r_

Bibliography

MOomrzt9VEFTpOtKJ9qlPAsO_qf81BsspBbh8rDzmCjJeeiAx6oC4_GuapqAq8CoM_QgjniJmhwO4E-_R1jxk8r9-0.

Library of Congress. "Adherents.com: Religion Statistics, Geography, Church Statistics." Web Archives, Aug. 9, 2007. www.loc.gov/item/lcwaN0003960/.

Marschall, Amy. "The Four Fear Responses: Fight, Flight, Freeze, and Fawn." Verywell Mind, Feb. 13, 2024. https://www.verywellmind.com/the-four-fear-responses-fight-flight-freeze-and-fawn-5205083.

Merriam Webster. "Runner's high." Last updated Aug. 10, 2024. https://www.merriam-webster.com/dictionary/runner%27s%20high.

Meta Religion. "The Rastafarian Religion." https://www.meta-religion.com/World_Religions/Other_religions/rastafarian_religion.htm.

National Spiritualist Association of Churches. "Religion: Principles and Objects." Beliefs, last updated Aug. 10, 2024.

New World Encyclopedia. "Animism: Common Features of Animism: Existence of Souls or Spirits." https://www.newworldencyclopedia.org/entry/animism.

The Noble Quran. Translated by Muhammad Muhsin Khân and Muhammad Taqî-ud-Dîn Al-Hilâlî. Madinah, K.S.A: Dar-us-Salam, 1419 AH.

Oxford Languages. "Belief." Last updated Aug. 10, 2024. https://www.google.com/search?q=believe+definition&rlz=1C1GCEA_enUS1080US1080&oq=believe+def&gs_lcrp=EgZjaHJvbWUqCggAEAAYsQMYgAQyCggAEAAYsQMYgAQyCQgBEEUYORiAB DIHCAIQABiABDIHCAMQABiABDIHCAQQABiABDIHCAUQABiABDIHCAY QABiABDIHCAcQABiABDIHCAgQABiABDIHCAkQABiA BNIBCDYxMTBqMG03qAIAsAIA&sourceid=chrome&ie=UTF-8.

———. "Cryonics." Last updated Aug. 11, 2024. https://www.google.com/search?q=cryonics+definition&rlz=1C1GCEA_enUS1080US1080&oq=cryonics&gs_lcrp=EgZjaHJvbWUqBwgCEAAYgAQyDAgAEEUYORixAxiABDIHCAEQABiABDIHC AIQABiABDINCAMQLhivARjHARiABDIHCAQQABiABDIHCAUQ ABiABDIHCAYQABiABDIHCAcQABiABDIHCAgQABiABDIHCAkQLhi ABNIBCDUzMjRqMG03qAIAsAIA&sourceid=chrome&ie=UTF-8.

———. "Desire." Last updated Aug. 10, 2024. https://www.google.com/search?q=desire+definition&rlz=1C1GCEA_enUS1080US1080&oq=desire&gs_lcrp=EgZjaHJvb WUqDwgBEAAYQxixAxiABBiKBTIRCAAQRRg5GEMYsQMYgAQYigUy DwgBEAAYQxixAxiABBiKBTIMCAIQABhDGIAEGIoFMgw IAxAAGEMYgAQYigUyDQgEEC4YgwEYsQMYgAQyDAgFEAAYQxiABBiKBTI HCAYQLhiABDIHCAcQABiABDIKCAgQABixAxiABDIHCAkQABiPAtIBCDU 2ODRqMG03qAIAsAIA&sourceid=chrome&ie=UTF-8.

———. "Win." Last updated Aug. 10, 2024. https://www.google.com/search?q=win+definition&rlz=1C1GCEA_enUS1080US1080&oq=win+def&gs_lcrp=EgZjaHJvbW UqBwgBEAAYgAQyCQgAEEUYORiABDIHCAEQABiABDIMCAIQABgKGLED GIAEMgcIAxAAGIAEMhIIBBAAGAoYgwEYsQMYgAQYigUyBwgFEA AYgAQyDwgGEAAYChiDARixAxiABDIHCAcQABiABDIJCAgQABgKGIA EMhIICRAAGAoYgwEYsQMYgAQYigXSAQg1NzE4ajBqN6gCALACAA& sourceid=chrome&ie=UTF-8.

Padmasambhava. *The Tibetan Book of the Dead.* New York: Penguin, 2006.

Patheos. "Baha'i: Beliefs—Afterlife and Salvation." Religion Library. http://www.patheos.com/Library/Bahai/Beliefs/Afterlife-and-Salvation?offset=1&max=1.

———. "Buddhism: Beliefs—Sacred Narratives." Religion Library. https://www.patheos.com/library/buddhism/beliefs.

Bibliography

———. "Christianity: Beliefs—Afterlife and Salvation." Religion Library. http://www.patheos.com/Library/Christianity/Beliefs/Afterlife-and-Salvation.html.

———. "Hinduism: Beliefs—Afterlife and Salvation." Religion Library. http://www.patheos.com/Library/Hinduism/Beliefs/Afterlife-and-Salvation.html.

———. "Islam: Beliefs—Afterlife and Salvation." Religion Library. http://www.patheos.com/Library/Islam/Beliefs/Afterlife-and-Salvation.html.

———. "Juche." Religion Library. http://www.patheos.com/Library/Juche.html.

———. "Judaism: Beliefs—Afterlife and Salvation." Religion Library. http://www.patheos.com/Library/Judaism/Beliefs/Afterlife-and-Salvation?offset=0&max=1.

———. "Scientology: Beliefs—Afterlife and Salvation." Religion Library. https://www.patheos.com/library/scientology/beliefs/afterlife-and-salvation.

———. "Shinto: Beliefs—Afterlife and Salvation." Religion Library. http://www.patheos.com/Library/Shinto/Beliefs/Afterlife-and-Salvation.html.

———. "Taoism: Beliefs—Afterlife and Salvation." Religion Library. http://www.patheos.com/Library/Taoism/Beliefs/Afterlife-and-Salvation.html.

———. "Unitarian-Universalism: Beliefs—Afterlife and Salvation." Religion Library. http://www.patheos.com/Library/Unitarian-Universalism/Beliefs/Afterlife-and-Salvation.html.

RealSikhism. "Quotations > Reincarnation." https://web.archive.org/web/20130630081849/http://www.realsikhism.com/index.php?action=quotes&topicid=12&topicname=Reincarnation.

Religion Facts. "Afterlife (Chinese Religion)." Chinese Traditional Religions. Mar. 27, 2015. Last updated June 21, 2024. http://www.religionfacts.com/chinese-religion/afterlife.

———. "Cao Dai Beliefs." Cao Dai. Oct. 24, 2016. Last updated June 21, 2024. https://religionfacts.com/cao-dai/beliefs.

———. "Christianity on the Afterlife." Christianity. Mar. 17, 2015. Last updated June 21, 2024. https://religionfacts.com/christianity/afterlife.

———. "Neopagan Beliefs." Neopaganism. Mar. 17, 2015. Last updated June 21, 2024. https://religionfacts.com/neopaganism/beliefs.

———. "Zoroastrian Beliefs." Zoroastrianism. Nov. 6, 2015. Last updated June 21, 2024. https://religionfacts.com/zoroastrianism/beliefs.

Richey, Jeffrey. "Confucianism: Beliefs—Afterlife and Salvation." Patheos: Religion Library. http://www.patheos.com/Library/Confucianism/Beliefs/Afterlife-and-Salvation?offset=1&max=1.

Robbins, Anthony. *Personal Power II: The Driving Force*. Vol. 12. San Diego, CA: Robbins Research International, 1996.

Robson, David. "Why We're so Terrified of the Unknown." *BBC News*, Oct. 26, 2021. https://www.bbc.com/worklife/article/20211022-why-were-so-terrified-of-the-unknown.

Rooke, Andrew. "Reincarnation in African Traditional Religion." World Spiritual Traditions: Theosophical Perspectives. http://www.theosophy-nw.org/theosnw/world/africa/af-rook2.htm.

"Shamanism Is Not a Religion, but Healing Based on Generosity." Faena Aleph. http://www.faena.com/aleph/articles/shamanism-is-not-a-religion-but-healing-based-on-generosity/.

Sikhi Wiki. "Sach Kand." Last updated Aug. 10, 2024. https://www.sikhiwiki.org/index.php/Sach_Khand.

Bibliography

Stuart, James. "Beliefs of the Zoroastrians on Hell." Classroom, Sept. 29, 2017. https://classroom.synonym.com/beliefs-of-the-zoroastrians-on-hell-12085986.html.

Taylor, Martin, and Smitha Bhandari. "What Does Fight, Flight, Freeze, Fawn Mean?" WebMD, last updated Aug. 25, 2024. https://www.webmd.com/mental-health/what-does-fight-flight-freeze-fawn-mean.

Tucker, Jim. *Return to Life: Extraordinary Cases of Children Who Remember Their Past Lives*. New York: St. Martin's, 2013.

Uniat, Lindsey. "Freshman Rowers Eligible for Varsity." *Yale News*, Sept. 11, 2012. https://yaledailynews.com/blog/2012/09/11/crew-freshman-rowers-eligible-for-varsity/.

Unitarian Universalist Association. "Leader Resource 3: Common Views Among Universalists." https://www.uua.org/re/tapestry/adults/newuu/workshop1/160230.shtml.

Van Wyk, I. W. C. "The Final Judgment in African Perspectives." *HTS* 62.2 (2006) 703–29. https://repository.up.ac.za/bitstream/handle/2263/14961/VanWyk_Final%282006%29.pdf?sequence=1.

Wikipedia. "2045 Initiative." Last updated Dec. 27, 2020. https://en.wikipedia.org/wiki/2045_Initiative.

———. "Alevism." Last updated Dec. 27, 2018. https://en.wikipedia.org/wiki/Alevism.

———. "Anattā." Last updated Feb. 4, 2020. https://en.wikipedia.org/wiki/Anatta.

———. "Bahá'í Faith on Life After Death." *Last updated July 28, 2019. https://en.wikipedia.org/wiki/Bah%C3%A1%27%C3%AD_Faith_on_life_after_death.*

———. "Bradley International Airport." Last updated June 26, 2021. https://en.wikipedia.org/wiki/Bradley_International_Airport.

———. "Buddhism." Last updated Dec. 21, 2018. https://en.wikipedia.org/wiki/Buddhism.

———. "Christian Universalism." Last updated Dec. 25, 2018. https://en.wikipedia.org/wiki/Christian_universalism.

———. "Copts." Last updated Dec. 27, 2018. https://en.wikipedia.org/wiki/Copts.

———. "Defence Mechanism." Last updated May 22, 2022. https://en.wikipedia.org/wiki/Defence_mechanism.

———. "Diyu." Last updated Aug. 17, 2024. https://en.wikipedia.org/wiki/Diyu.

———. "Druze." Last updated Dec. 27, 2018. https://en.wikipedia.org/wiki/Druze.

———. "Forgiveness." Last updated July 7, 2021. https://en.wikipedia.org/wiki/Forgiveness.

———. "God in Jainism." Last updated Nov. 25, 2018. https://en.wikipedia.org/wiki/God_in_Jainism.

———. "Habit." Last updated Jan. 29, 2022. https://en.wikipedia.org/wiki/Habit.

———. "Hinduism." Last updated Mar. 26, 2019. https://en.wikipedia.org/wiki/Hinduism.

———. "John F. Kennedy International Airport." Last updated June 26, 2021. https://en.wikipedia.org/wiki/John_F._Kennedy_International_Airport.

———. "John McEnroe." Last updated Aug. 28, 2021. https://en.wikipedia.org/wiki/John_McEnroe.

———. "Karma Yoga." Last updated Jan. 23, 2021. https://en.wikipedia.org/wiki/Karma_yoga#:~:text=Of%20the%20paths%20to%20spiritual,Bhagavad%20Gita%2C%20purifies%20the%20mind.

———. "List of Religious Populations." Last updated Dec. 1, 2018. https://en.wikipedia.org/wiki/List_of_religious_populations.

Bibliography

———. "Mind." Last updated Dec. 22, 2012. http://en.wikipedia.org/wiki/Mind.

———. "Mind-Body Problem." Last updated Sept. 12, 2024. https://en.wikipedia.org/wiki/Mind%E2%80%93body_problem.

———. "Pascal's Wager." Last updated Feb. 1, 2020. https://en.wikipedia.org/wiki/Pascal%27s_wager.

———. "Payne Whitney Gymnasium." Last updated June 20, 2021. https://en.wikipedia.org/wiki/Payne_Whitney_Gymnasium.

———. "Phillips Academy." Last updated Mar. 28, 2022. https://en.wikipedia.org/wiki/Phillips_Academy.

———. "Rastafari." Last updated Nov. 4, 2018. https://en.wikipedia.org/wiki/Rastafari.

———. "Rowing (Sport)." Last updated June 20, 2021. https://en.wikipedia.org/wiki/Rowing_(sport).

———. "Saṃsāra (Buddhism)." Last updated Dec. 21, 2018. https://en.wikipedia.org/wiki/Sa%E1%B9%83s%C4%81ra_(Buddhism).

———. "Self-Actualization." Last updated Nov. 26, 2021. https://en.wikipedia.org/wiki/Self-actualization#Abraham_Maslow's_concept_of_self-actualization.

———. "Self-Transcendence." Last updated June 25, 2022. https://en.wikipedia.org/wiki/Self-transcendence.

———. "Serenity Prayer." Last updated Apr. 14, 2022. https://en.wikipedia.org/wiki/Serenity_Prayer.

———. "Shamanism." Last updated Jan. 24, 2021. https://en.wikipedia.org/wiki/Shamanism.

———. "*Shirk* (Islam)." Last updated Aug. 16, 2024. https://en.wikipedia.org/wiki/Shirk_(Islam).

———. "Spiritualism." Last updated July 19, 2018. https://en.wikipedia.org/wiki/Spiritualism.

———. "The Summerland." Last updated Oct. 11, 2011. http://en.wikipedia.org/wiki/The_Summerland.

———. "Technological Singularity." Last updated Dec. 7, 2020. https://en.wikipedia.org/wiki/Technological_singularity.

———. "Tenrikyo Anthropology." Last updated Jan. 25, 2021. https://en.wikipedia.org/wiki/Tenrikyo_anthropology.

———. "Terror Management Theory." Last updated Apr. 17, 2022. https://en.wikipedia.org/wiki/Terror_management_theory#cite_note-10.

———. "Transhumanism." Last updated Dec. 27, 2020. https://en.wikipedia.org/wiki/Transhumanism.

———. "Unitarian Universalism." Last updated Nov. 11, 2018. https://en.wikipedia.org/wiki/Unitarian_Universalism.

Wiktionary. "Metathesiophobia." Last updated Aug. 12, 2024. https://en.wiktionary.org/wiki/metathesiophobia.

Wilson, Anne, et al. "My Jesus." Copyright ã 2021 by Jacobs Story Music, Capitol CMG.

Yahoo! Answers. "What Is the Shintoism Belief about Afterlife? Anonymous: Favorite Answer." https://web.archive.org/web/20210422002106/http://answers.yahoo.com/question/index?qid=20081108090138AAnFvwn.

Zammit, Victor J. "How Different Religions View the Afterlife." http://www.victorzammit.com/articles/religions3.html.

Appendix A

Major Religions of the World
Ranked by Number of Adherents

The information contained here in appendix A is taken from Adherents.com. The figures presented for each religion should not be viewed as exact numbers, but rather directionally correct. They are valid for determining a relative size/ranking of the religion in relation to all other religions.[1]

1. Christianity: 2.1 billion
2. Islam: 1.5 billion
3. Secular/Nonreligious/Agnostic/Atheist: 1.1 billion
4. Hinduism: 900 million
5. Chinese Traditional Religion: 394 million
6. Buddhism: 376 million
7. Primal-Indigenous: 300 million
8. African Traditional and Diasporic: 100 million
9. Sikhism: 23 million
10. Juche: 19 million
11. Spiritism: 15 million
12. Judaism: 14 million
13. Bahá'í: 7 million
14. Jainism: 4.2 million

1. Library of Congress, Adherents.com.

15. Shinto: 4 million
16. Cao Dai: 4 million
17. Zoroastrianism: 2.6 million
18. Tenrikyo: 2 million
19. Neo-Paganism: 1 million
20. Unitarian Universalism: 800 thousand
21. Rastafarianism: 600 thousand
22. Scientology: 500 thousand

INTRODUCTION

The adherent counts presented in the list above are current estimates of the number of people who have at least a minimal level of self-identification as adherents of the religion. Levels of participation vary within all groups. These numbers tend toward the high end of reasonable worldwide estimates. Valid arguments can be made for different figures, but if the same criteria are used for all groups, the relative order should be the same. Further details and sources are available below and in the Adherents.com main database.

A major source for these estimates is the detailed country-by-country analysis done by David B. Barrett's religious statistics organization, whose data are published in the *Encyclopedia Britannica* (including annual updates and yearbooks) and also in the *World Christian Encyclopedia* (the latest edition of which—published in 2001—has been consulted). Hundreds of additional sources providing more thorough and detailed research about individual religious groups have also been consulted.

This listing is not a comprehensive list of all religions, only the "major" ones (as defined below). There are distinct religions other than the ones listed above. But this list accounts for the religions of over 98 percent of the world's population. Below are listed some religions which are in this listing (including Mandeans, PL Kyodan, Ch'ondogyo, Vodoun, New Age, Seicho-No-Ie, Falun Dafa/Falun Gong, Taoism, Roma), along with explanations for why they do not qualify as "major world religions" on this list. Hence, in this list, which is explicitly statistical and sociological in perspective, Taoism should be thought of as a major branch of Chinese traditional religion.

Appendix A

This world religions listing is derived from the statistics data in the Adherents.com database. The list was created by the same people who collected data for and organized this database, in consultation with university professors of comparative religions and scholars from different religions. We invite additional input. The Adherents.com collection of religious adherent statistics now has over 43,000 adherent statistic citations, for over 4,300 different faith groups, covering all countries of the world. This is not an absolutely exhaustive compilation of all such data, but it is by far the largest compilation available on the internet. Various academic researchers and religious representatives regularly share documented adherent statistics with Adherents.com so that their information can be available in a centralized database.

Statistics and geography citations for religions *not* on this list, as well as subgroups within these religions (such as Catholics, Protestants, Karaites, Wiccans, Shiites, etc.) can be found in the main Adherents.com database.

PARAMETERS OF THIS LIST

In order to rank religions by size, two parameters must be defined:

1. What constitutes a "religion"?
2. How is "size" determined?

With a working definition of "a religion" and a method for measuring size, criteria for what constitutes a "major" religion must be determined, otherwise this list could be impractically inclusive and long.

"Major religions," for the purposes of this list, are:

- Large—at least 500,000 adherents
- Widespread—appreciable numbers of members live and worship in more than just one country or limited region
- Independent—the religion is clearly independent and distinct from a broader religion

Appendix B

Afterlife Beliefs of Major Religions of the World.

1. Christianity

Christian beliefs about the afterlife vary between denominations and individual Christians, but the vast majority of Christians believe in some kind of heaven, in which the deceased enjoy the presence of God and loved ones for eternity. Views differ as to what is required to get to heaven, and conceptions of heaven differ as well.

A slightly smaller majority of Christians believe in hell, a place of suffering where unbelievers or sinners are punished. Views differ as to whether hell is eternal and whether its punishment is spiritual or physical. Some Christians reject the notion altogether.

Catholic Christians also believe in purgatory, a temporary place of punishment for Christians who have died with un-confessed sins.[1]

Most Christians look to the New Testament for guidance on afterlife beliefs.

In his letter to the Romans, Paul wrote, "For the wages of sin is death, but the gift of God is eternal life in Christ Jesus our Lord" (Romans 6:23). This single sentence neatly summarizes the Christian doctrine of atonement, which teaches that the reconciliation of sinful humanity with the God of love was accomplished by God in the sacrifice of His son, Jesus Christ, on the cross. . . .

---

1. Religion Facts, "Christianity on the Afterlife."

Appendix B

> Branches of Christianity differ on how humans can and are to respond to this gift of God, but all Christians agree that the resurrection of Jesus made eternal life possible for humans....
>
> Most importantly, Christian belief about salvation holds that eternal life cannot be earned by human striving, because no one would deserve salvation if judged entirely on merit. Eternal life is a gift from God.[2]

2. Islam

Muslims believe in a final judgment, referred to by many names in the Qur'an: the Day of Reckoning, the Day of Distress, the Day of the Gathering, the Great Announcement, and the Hour. Common with other theologies that subscribe to the idea of a judgment, they also believe in heaven (often referred to in the Qur'an as paradise or "gardens of pleasure") and hell. Each person is responsible for the judgment he or she will receive. People are judged based on their intentions and their deeds.

> Islam does not teach that we are in need of intercession, although some traditions have allowed that Muhammad might intercede with God on our behalf. No one can know God, but at the same time, no one stands between the individual Muslim and God. If we find that we have sinned, we may sincerely apologize, and through our remorse, receive forgiveness. The slate is clean, and we may begin again. This will likely happen to us many times in our lives, because we are not perfect. But on the Last Day, there are no excuses. God has sent many prophets to remind us of our duty and to wake us up when we forget our dependence on God. As a result, the punishment on the Last Day is just.[3]

Foundational to Islam is the concept of personal accountability, where we are responsible for the reward or punishment received in the next life.

> A person's ultimate destiny, whether it is heaven or hell, depends on the degree to which that person intended and acted as God desires, with justice and mercy toward others. While it is impossible to know with certainty who will go to heaven and hell, believers ... may hope for heaven. There is some evidence that nonbelievers can attain paradise.[4]

2. Patheos, "Christianity."
3. Patheos, "Islam."
4. Patheos, "Islam."

However, Islam teaches there is one great sin which will not be forgiven by God (known to Muslims as Allah). This unpardonable sin is Shirk. In Islam, Shirk is the sin of idolatry or polytheism, which assigns or establishes partners with Allah or ascribes divine attributes for worship to others besides Allah. Individuals who commit this sin also believe that their source of power, harm, and blessings comes from others besides Allah, the one singular God, who has no children or wives, according to Islam.[5]

The Qur'an states:

> Verily, Allah forgives not that partners should be set up with Him (in worship), but He forgives except that (anything else) to whom He wills; and whoever sets up partners with Allah in worship, he has indeed invented a tremendous sin. (4:48)

3. Secular/Nonreligious/Agnostic/Atheist

"This is a highly disparate group and not a single religion."[6] So, there is no consistent belief in an afterlife. In general people who fall within this group do not believe in God or an afterlife. To help describe this group's followers, below is a list of definitions for some of the various classifications.

> "Agnostic" in normal usage today means "don't know" or having an open mind about religious belief, especially the existence of gods. It can also mean something much firmer: that nothing is known, or can possibly be known, about gods or other supernatural phenomena, and that it is wrong of people to claim otherwise. That is the original meaning of the word, and 19th century "agnostics" lived their lives atheistically in practice—that is, without any reference to any concepts of gods.
>
> "Atheist" (literally meaning 'without gods') includes those who reject a belief in the existence of a god or gods and those who simply choose to live without a god or gods. Along with this often, but not always, go disbelief in the soul, an afterlife, and other beliefs arising from god-based religions.
>
> "Freethinker" is an old-fashioned term, popular in the nineteenth century, used of those who reject authority in matters of belief, especially political and religious beliefs. It was a very popular term in the 19th century and is still used in different languages

---

5. Wikipedia, "*Shirk* (Islam)."
6. Library of Congress, Adherents.com.

Appendix B

in some European countries by non-religious organisations to describe themselves.

"Humanist" is used today to mean those who seek to live good lives without religious or superstitious beliefs. A humanist may embrace all or most of the other approaches introduced here, and in addition humanists believe that moral values follow on from human nature and experience in some way. Humanists base their moral principles on reason (which leads them to reject the idea of any supernatural agency), on shared human values and respect for others. They believe that people should work together to improve the quality of life for all and make it more equitable. Humanism is a full philosophy, "life stance" or worldview, rather than being about one aspect of religion, knowledge, or politics.

"Non-religious"—as well as those who are uninterested in religion or who reject it, this category may include the vague or unaffiliated, those who are only nominally or culturally affiliated to a religious tradition, and the superstitious.

"Rationalist" in this context, describing a non-religious belief, means someone who prioritises the use of reason and considers reason crucial in investigating and understanding the world. Rationalists usually reject religion on the grounds that it is unreasonable. (Rationalism is in contradistinction to fideism—positions which rely on or advocate "faith" in some degree).

"Skeptic" today usually means someone who doubts the truth of religious and other supernatural or "paranormal" beliefs, typically on rationalist grounds. ('Skeptic' also has a special philosophical meaning: someone who rejects or is skeptical with regard to all claims to knowledge).

"Secularists" believe that laws and public institutions (for example, the education system) should be neutral as between alternative religions and beliefs. Almost all humanists are secularists, but religious believers may also take a secularist position which calls for freedom of belief, including the right to change belief and not to believe. Secularists seek to ensure that persons and organisations are neither privileged nor disadvantaged by virtue of their religion or lack of it. They believe secular laws—those that apply to all citizens—should be the product of a democratic process, and should not be determined, or unduly influenced, by religious leaders or religious texts. The word "secularism" was once used to describe a non-religious worldview more generally (sometimes described in similar terms to humanism) but this original meaning is very old-fashioned and has fallen completely out of use.[7]

---

7. Humanists UK, "Non-religious Beliefs."

4. Hinduism

"While Hinduism has been called the oldest religion in the world, many practitioners refer to their religion as Sanātana Dharma ('the eternal way'), which refers to the idea that its origins lie beyond human history, as revealed in the Hindu texts."[8]

One of the fundamental principles of Hinduism is the concept of samsara, the cycle of birth, life, death, and rebirth. Humans are reborn over and over. They can, however, "escape" rebirth by ridding themselves of karma and attaining moksha—the end of delusion. In some Hindu schools of thought, attaining moksha will not only end samsara, but will also bring benefits to the individual in her current lifetime. The person will be able to live a more complete, satisfying, and rewarding life.

The Bhagavad Gita states:

> As a person puts on new clothes and discards old and torn clothes, similarly an embodied soul enters new material bodies, leaving the old bodies. (BG 2:22)

Hinduism did not begin with a goal of helping its followers attain salvation and in fact had very little commentary on what happens after death.

> In the earliest strata of Hinduism, the Vedas [the most ancient of the world's Scriptures], there is very little discussion of the afterlife. . . .
>
> Some in the Vedic world eventually set out . . . to find . . . a path that would lead to eternal salvation. . . .
>
> According to the Upanishads . . . when there is no karma, there is no rebirth. One is released. . . .
>
> This path . . . of knowledge, is not the only means to attain . . . salvation. . . .
>
> The Bhagavad Gita introduces the path of devotion. . . . One can attain salvation through selfless loving devotion to a chosen god.[9]

Another way to salvation is along the path of action.

> Of the paths to spiritual liberation in Hinduism, karma yoga is the path of unselfish action. It teaches that a spiritual seeker should act according to dharma, without being attached to the fruits or personal consequences. Karma Yoga, states the

---

8. Wikipedia, "Hinduism."
9. Patheos, "Hinduism."

Appendix B

Bhagavad Gita, purifies the mind. It leads one to consider dharma of work, and the work according to one's dharma, doing god's work and in that sense becoming and being "like unto god Krishna" in every moment of one's life.

According to LORD Krishna in Bhagavad Gita, Karma yoga is the spiritual practice of "selfless action performed for the benefit of others." Karma yoga is a path to reach moksha (spiritual liberation) through work. It is rightful action without being attached to fruits or being manipulated by what the results might be, a dedication to one's duty, and trying one's best while being neutral to rewards or outcomes such as success or failure.[10]

5. Chinese Traditional (Confucianism, Taoism, and Chinese Folk Religions)

Confucianism

Kongzi stated that the afterlife was beyond human comprehension. Humans should live and behave in such a way as to promote ideal social relations, rather than to act based on the expectations of rewards or punishments after death. In Confucian terms, a meaningful life is one in which one develops one's innate moral potential to the fullest while fulfilling all of one's social obligations. At the same time, from a Confucian perspective, one cannot live fully in the present without being fully responsible to the past, both in terms of paying respect to one's ancestors and making the best of what they have left behind. What happens to human beings after they die is less important to Confucian thinkers than how the living fulfill their obligations to the dead.[11]

Leading Confucian practitioners have elaborated on the foundational tenets of the religion.

In *Centrality and Commonality: An Essay on Confucian Religiousness* (SUNY Press 1989), the contemporary "New Confucian" thinker Tu Weiming describes the religious dimension of Confucianism: "Being religious, in the Confucian perspective ... means being engaged in the process of learning to be fully human. We can define the Confucian

10. Wikipedia, "Karma yoga."
11. Richey, "Confucianism."

way of being religious as ultimate self-transformation as a communal act and as a faithful dialogical response to the transcendent." This lifetime process of ultimate self-transformation requires both membership in community (starting with a human family) and individual engagement with the source of ultimate meaning, *Tian*. Although Mengzi's vision of Confucianism largely established the parameters of Confucian spirituality for all subsequent generations, it was the work of his interpreter Zhu Xi that articulated most influentially what it means to live religiously as a Confucian.

Zhu saw the universe as constantly involved in a dynamic creative process of interplay between *li* (cosmic principle, including principles of morality, social order, etc.) and *qi* (vital energy, but also the material world in its tangible forms). For Zhu, the human heart-mind is where li and qi meet, become one, and help order the universe: "The heart-mind unites nature (i.e., qi) and emotion (i.e., li)." From a Confucian perspective, one can play no more important role than to co-create moral order in the cosmos. The proper unity of human nature with moral sentiments leads, through the discipline of Confucian self-cultivation, to the desired goal of *cheng* (authenticity or sincerity) as manifested in *he* (harmony) and *zhong* (centeredness) revealed through an exemplary moral life. In such a life, a Confucian sees both salvation here and now (in the sense that one has attained the Confucian goal of actualizing one's innate, Tian-given and Tian-identified, potential) and eternal life hereafter (in the sense that one becomes an example and model for others who seek to walk the Confucian path of self-transformation).[12]

Taoism

Early Taoism focused on this worldly goal of achieving immortality of the physical body. Later, in reaction to Buddhism, Taoism incorporated concepts of heaven, hell, and rebirth.

> In no area is the lack of a . . . unified Taoist belief system more evident than in . . . concepts about the afterlife and salvation. . . .
> Taoist notions of life beyond death are . . . discerned by looking at the time prior to the establishment of Buddhism in China.

---

12. Richey, "Confucianism."

Appendix B

> Salvation ... is a matter of participation in the eternal return of the natural world, a yielding to chaos followed by spontaneous creation, in a never-ending cycle.[13]

Chinese Folk Religions

> The concept of the "Ten Courts of Yanluo" (十殿閻羅) began after Chinese folk religion was influenced by Buddhism. In this variation of Chinese mythology, there are 12,800 hells located under the earth—eight dark hells, eight cold hells and 84,000 miscellaneous hells located at the edge of the universe. All will go to Diyu after death but the period of time one spends in Diyu is not forever—it depends on the severity of the sins one committed. After receiving due punishment, one will eventually be sent for reincarnation. Diyu is divided into ten courts, each overseen by a Yanwang. Souls pass from stage to stage at the decision of a different judge. The "Ten Courts of Yanluo" is also known as the Ten Courts of Yanwang (十殿阎王), Ten Lords of Minggong (冥宫十王), Ten Courts of Yanjun (十殿阎君), Ten-Lords of Difu (地府十王), and Ten-Lords of Mingfu (冥府十王).[14]

Many beliefs, practices, and traditions—some complementary and some conflicting—are grouped into what is commonly referred to as Chinese folk religions.

> Over the years, diverse Chinese myths and beliefs have gotten lumped into the nebulous category of "folk religion." This category includes everything from Traditional Chinese Medicine to beliefs about yin and yang. In pre-Buddhist Northern Chinese beliefs, everyone's soul had two parts, the *po* (the yin soul, made of earth) and the *hun* (the yang soul, made of *qi*.) Both souls needed sustenance to live and when the souls died, they went to different places, with the *hun* going to heaven in earliest ideas, and the *po* staying with the body or going to the underworld (although neither was specified as a place of reward or punishment.)
>
> Heaven (天, tiān) is considered the source of all moral meaning and good, and it is the place where many gods reside (including the first god, the Jade Emperor.) Traditional Chinese religion honors many gods, and a few preside specifically over the dead, including the

13. Patheos, "Taoism."
14. Wikipedia, "Diyu."

demigod Zhong Kui who subdues evil spirits and recruits them for a ghost army.[15]

6. Buddhism

There is no consistent notion of the afterlife or salvation in Buddhism. It varies according to country, era, and individual perspective.

> Buddhism began as a way to address the suffering that exists in the world and was not overly-focused on ultimate salvation. That said, however, there was a clear doctrine of salvation in the Buddha's teachings: Salvation in early Buddhism was nirvana, the extinguishing of the all karma that constitutes the self. Nirvana is not a place or a state, but the end of rebirth.
>
> Significantly, the Buddha said little about nirvana, because he felt that the alleviation of suffering was far more important, and that focusing on the goal of ultimate salvation would only lead to more attachments, and therefore more suffering. Rather than focus on nirvana as a goal, therefore, lay Buddhists were encouraged to give donations of goods, services, or money to monks or monasteries; to chant or copy sutras; and to engage in other activities in order to gain merit that could lead to a more desirable rebirth, which would bring them closer to enlightenment.
>
> Some Mahayana Buddhist monks aspired to become bodhisattvas, postponing the dissolution of self until all living things are enlightened. For seminal religious figures and heads of religious orders in Tibet, this took the unusual form of continued incarnations in human form as the same individual, lifetime after lifetime.
> . . .
> The notion of skillful means in Mahayana Buddhism led to other interpretations of salvation, such as rebirth in a Pure Land, where one could continue to aspire to enlightenment in pleasant surroundings without fear of rebirth in human form. Mahayana texts also refer to hells into which one might be reborn, usually in the context of rescuing others from a hellish domain or transferring merit to those in such a place. There is also reference in the earliest texts to Yama, a deity of death who will judge and punish those who do evil. The punishment is not eternal but lasts until the karma of these misdeeds has been exhausted.
>
> As Buddhism evolved and as it moved to other countries with different religious backgrounds, other views of the afterlife emerged. Yama became a central figure in popular understandings

15. Bullock, "What Happens When You Die?"

Appendix B

of the afterlife in East Asia and also in Tibet. Tibetan Buddhists also envisioned the Bardo, a kind of limbo where the soul or self remained until the next rebirth....

Notions of heavens and hells eventually became a part of popular Buddhism throughout Asia. These range from ideal surroundings such as the Pure Lands to horrific worlds of punishment and suffering....

As should be evident, there is no single, consistent notion of the afterlife and salvation within Buddhism. There are diverse and contradictory ideas even within individual countries. This is the result of the merging of Buddhism with pre-existing conceptions, of contradictions between scholarly and popular understandings, and of the evolution of ideas within Buddhism throughout the life of the religion.[16]

While there are different and specific aspects of Buddhist beliefs from various regions, most Buddhist traditions share the goal of overcoming suffering and ending the cycle of birth, death, and rebirth. This is achieved either by the attainment of nirvana or through the path of Buddhahood. The way to reach this ultimate state can vary. In addition, rebirth can take place in the physical world or in another more ideal, peaceful place (e.g., Pure Lands). There may or may not be a temporary visit to a place of punishment to atone for the bad karma generated in one's most recent life/incarnation. The path most often taught is the Noble Eightfold Path.

7. **Primal-Indigenous (Ethno-religionist, Animists, and Shamanists)**

   Ethno-religionist

   Many distinct religions are included in the ethno-religionist category. And, as such, there are many different views of the afterlife. These views cover a broad spectrum of beliefs from the concept of nirvana, heaven (paradise) and hell, heaven only and no hell, no heaven and no hell, to the belief that bad souls are lost, extinguished, destroyed or simply cease to exist. Some of the ethnic groups included in this category include the Druze of the Levant, the Copts of Egypt, the Yazidi of northern Iraq, the Alevis of Turkey and the Yarsan [also known as Ahl-e Haqq] found primarily in western Iran and Iraq.[17]

---

16. Patheos, "Buddhism."
17. Library of Congress, Adherents.com.

The Druze

Reincarnation is a paramount principle in the Druze faith. Reincarnations occur instantly at one's death because there is an eternal duality of the body and the soul and it is impossible for the soul to exist without the body. A human soul will transfer only to a human body, in contrast to the Hindu and Buddhist belief systems, according to which souls can transfer to any living creature. Furthermore, a male Druze can be reincarnated only as another male Druze and a female Druze only as another female Druze. A Druze cannot be reincarnated in the body of a non-Druze. Additionally, souls cannot be divided and the number of souls existing in the universe is finite. The cycle of rebirth is continuous and the only way to escape is through successive reincarnations. When this occurs, the soul is united with the Cosmic Mind and achieves the ultimate happiness.[18]

The Copts

The Copts are an ethnoreligious group indigenous to Northeast Africa who primarily inhabit the area of modern Egypt, where they are the largest Christian denomination in the country and in the Middle East.[19]

The Yazidi (Also Spelled Yezidi)

Yazidis believe that the world was created by God, who entrusted it to seven angels led by one known as the Peacock Angel, also called Melek Taus. Melek Taus is the primary figure in the Yazidi belief system, as he filled the earth with flora and fauna.

Their religion is monotheistic and non-dualistic, and they do not believe in the concept of Hell. For them, all people have good and evil inside of them, and choices are made free of external temptation. They believe in internal purification through metempsychosis, a term referring to the transmigration of souls, according to Encyclopedia Britannica. They believe that the seven angels are occasionally reincarnated in human form.

---

18. Wikipedia, "Druze."
19. Wikipedia, "Copts."

Appendix B

Yazidis believe that they are descended directly from Adam alone, while the rest of humanity comes from the lineage of both Adam and Eve.[20]

The Alevis

Despite different descriptions of God within the Alevi religion, there is no evidence found of God ruling based on fear. Accordingly, God will not judge people by their acts of worship. There is also no literal heaven or hell with material pleasures or punishments.

> Alevis believe in the immortality of the soul. Alevis, who believe in a literal existence of supernatural beings, also believe in good and bad angels (melekler). Alevis believe in Satan who is the one that encourages human's evil desires (nefs). Alevis believe in an existence of spiritual creatures such as the Jinns (Cinler) and the evil eye.[21]

The Yarsan (Also Known as Ahl-e Haqq)

There is no concept of heaven or hell in the Yarsan religion.

> Everyone has the essence of god, or bounty of god; some have many and some like only to taste it.
>
> Incarnation and evolution are two separate issues and most scholars, philosophers, and Yārsānis reject incarnation with respect to a certain quality followed by Incarnations. They believe in evolution, rather than incarnation. As scholars of Yārsāni have stated, each human being needs to pass 1000 worlds in order to reach the last 1001st, stage, i.e., eternal perfection. Accordingly, each creature, depending on its stance, moves from one body to another in order to complete perfection.
>
> The concepts and beliefs of Yārsān presented here have concentrated on the soul showing its Divine Essence. Therefore, the following features can be reported in brief for Doon-ā Doon in the Yārsānism School: First, a soul, depending on its talents and gifts, moves from one body to another—that of a human being, an animal, or other. Second, a soul is expected to pass 1001 epochs in varying worlds to reach and achieve perfection; again, the

20. Hafiz, "Yazidi Beliefs and Cosmology."
21. Wikipedia, "Alevism."

quiddity and quality of this procedure depends on his/her deeds, behavior and talent. Third, the soul who reaches the 1001st body in fact reaches the Truth "Haghighat" stage, or the "great happiness" (also called *Zāte Heq* or God). This means that a soul is in the last epoch of a mundane life. Lastly, a soul will experience the resurrection. What differentiates these beliefs from Incarnations, is that incarnation is without definite time but according to Manichean, the target is followed by these Trans carnations' reach to Land of lighting. Most scholars who considered Doon-ā-Doon and incarnation in Manichean (Parthian zādmūrd) the same have neglected this considerable difference. It's worth noting that according to my interview with a Yārsāni member, I understand that Yārsānism upholds that all individuals have the essence of God, and in the end the soul reaches Sultan Sahak. Yet, another great difference between Manichaeism and Yārsān.[22]

Animists

> The cornerstone of animistic thought is the affirmation of the existence of some kind of metaphysical entities (such as souls or spirits) that are seen as the life-source (or life-force) of human beings, animals, plants and even non-living objects and phenomena. For animistic cultures, the existence of these entities (with their respective operational and volitional qualities) provides explanations for the innumerable changes witnessed in both the natural world and the human world.[23]

While animists can have different beliefs about the fate of one's life-source at the time of physical death, it is widely accepted that it continues to exist.

> Most animistic belief systems hold that this spirit survives physical death. In some instances, the spirit is believed to pass into a more leisurely world of abundant game and ever-ripe crops, while in other systems, such as that of the Navajo religion, the spirit remains on earth as a ghost, often becoming malignant in the process. Still other systems combine these two beliefs, holding that the afterlife involves a journey to the spirit world upon which the soul must not become lost. This journey entails much wandering as a ghost. The correct performance of funerary rites, mourning

22. Hosseini, "Death in Yārsān."
23. New World Encyclopedia, "Animism."

Appendix B

rituals, and ancestor worship were often considered necessary for expediting the deceased soul's completion of this journey.[24]

Shamanists

Shamanism is a system of religious practice. Historically, it is often associated with indigenous and tribal societies, and involves belief that shamans, with a connection to the otherworld, have the power to heal the sick, communicate with spirits, and escort souls of the dead to the afterlife. It is an ideology that used to be widely practiced in Europe, Asia, North and South America, and Africa. It centered on the belief in supernatural phenomenon such as the world of gods, demons, and ancestral spirits.[25]

There is no single agreed-upon definition for the word shamanism or for the practice of it.

There are many variations of shamanism throughout the world, but several common beliefs are shared by all forms of shamanism. Common beliefs identified by Eliade (1972) are the following:

- Spirits exist and they play important roles both in individual lives and in human society.
- The shaman can communicate with the spirit world.
- Spirits can be benevolent or malevolent.
- The shaman can treat sickness caused by malevolent spirits.
- The shaman can employ trances inducing techniques to incite visionary ecstasy and go on vision quests.
- The shaman's spirit can leave the body to enter the supernatural world to search for answers.
- The shaman evokes animal images as spirit guides, omens, and message-bearers.
- The shaman can perform other varied forms of divination, scry, throw bones or runes, and sometimes foretell of future events.[26]

---

24. New World Encyclopedia, "Animism."
25. Wikipedia, "Shamanism."
26. Wikipedia, "Shamanism."

Although included in the list by Adherents.com and commonly identified as a "religion," "it is important to highlight that shamanism is not a religion, and neither does it demand that one believe in the shaman's worldview. Faith is a judicial demand introduced by Christianity, but in shamanism, spirits and gods exist with the knowledge that, for others, buildings, animals and people exist."[27]

8. African Traditional and Diasporic

Discussing African notions of afterlife necessitates several preliminary and pertinent observations.

First, Africa is characterized by a tremendous ethnic and cultural diversity. There are about three thousand African ethnic groups, each boasting a distinctive common history, culture, language, and recognizable belief system. . . .

Across the many ethnic groupings and cultural expressions, however, one can discern commonalities in worldviews that make it possible to speak of an "African" worldview as compared, say, to a "Hindu" one. Summarizing distinctive markers of this African worldview, Sambuli Mosha isolates four key ideas, namely: (1) the centrality of belief in God, (2) an acknowledgment of the intrinsic unity between individuals and communities, (3) viewing the universe as an interconnected, interdependent whole, (4) embracing life as a process of spiritual formation and transformation (Mosha, 2000). All these markers shape the way Africans conceptualize both this life and the hereafter.

Secondly, African beliefs are *dynamic* rather than static. They are shaped and influenced by other belief systems that they encounter in history. While this dynamism is manifest in all aspects of belief, here we focus on concepts of the hereafter. In this regard, we note for example that ancient Egyptians held very clear eschatological ideas featuring notions of heaven and hell and a final judgment. Thus, in the Egyptian *Book of the Dead*, a text designed to be a guide for the soul as it journeyed on beyond physical death, Osiris determines the destiny of the dead. Having measured their moral worth against the feather of Maat (symbolizing truth and justice), he sends them "west," to the "abode of the righteous," or to "hell." Today, the pyramids where the pharaohs, ancient Egyptian kings believed to be immortal, were entombed remain an enduring testimony of the ancient Egyptians' preoccupation with life after death.

27. Aleph, "Shamanism."

Appendix B

Two thousand years later, these Egyptian ideas of the hereafter were part of the repertoire of beliefs in circulation in the Mediterranean world as Christianity was taking shape. Later still, in the nineteenth century, through Christian missionaries these ideas found their way into sub-Saharan Africa. Here, they reinforced prior indigenous concepts of the afterlife where these were already incorporated notions of a final judgment, as in the case of the Yoruba of Nigeria and LoDagaa of Ghana (Ray, 1976, pp. 143ff). Elsewhere, for example among the Agikuyu of Kenya, ideas of heaven and hell were introduced de novo.... Among the Gikuyu, as was typical in most indigenous African communities, though one's moral misconduct could provoke divine anger and punishment, such punishment was this-worldly rather than delayed and otherworldly.[28]

Given the cultural and historical diversity across the great continent, it is reasonable to expect that not all Africans hold the same belief about the fate of souls after physical death.

Traditional Africans believe in a life after death for their ancestors but are not aware of rewards or punishment in the afterlife (Mbiti 1975a:259–262; 1985:161; Sundermeier 1990:154; Hammond-Tooke 1993:149). Theo Sundermeier (1990:154, 201), however, notes two exceptions. The Koko and Basa peoples of Cameroon believe that evil people are destined for a cold place and good people for a place full of light. In view of the fact that they also believe that the repenters are destined for an intermediate state of existence, the originality of their beliefs is, however, doubtful. The Akan people of Ghana (according to Sundermeier) is the other exception. They believe in reward and punishment after life. The rest of Africa believes in a God that judges and punishes evildoers in the here and now during their earthly life, but not after death. John Mbiti (1975a:259–262; 1985:161) also refers to some exceptions to the rule. In this regard he mentions the Yoruba who believe in a judgment after death, based on earthly morality and the Lodagaa who fear punishment of evil by the ancestors after death. He also refers to, the Lozi who believe that eternal life (or life with the ancestors) will only be granted when people could identify themselves to the ancestors through tribal marks on their arms. Therefore, as far as we know this epithet of God is, apart from these exceptions, unknown to traditional Africa. Steve Biko (2004:49) affirms this when he, as a Christian traditionalist, states:

---

28. Hinga, "Afterlife."

> "We believed—and this was consistent with our views of life—that all people who died had a special place next to God. We felt that a communication with God could only be through these people. We never knew anything about hell—we do not believe that God can create people only to punish them eternally after a short period on earth … It was the missionaries who confused our people with their religion. They … preach a theology of the existence of hell, scaring our fathers and mothers with stories about burning in eternal flames and gnashing of teeth and grinding of bone. This cold cruel religion was strange to us but our fore-fathers [sic!] were sufficiently scared of the unknown impending [d]anger to believe that it was worth a try. Down went our cultural values!"[29]

Although not at the forefront of ideologies when discussing traditional African religions, reincarnation is a foundational belief.

> It is not widely realized, however, that reincarnation is an essential tenet of many traditional African religious systems and philosophies. Belief in rebirth has been reported amongst peoples scattered the length and breadth of the mighty continent: Akamba (Kenya), Akan (Ghana), Lango (Uganda), Luo (Zambia), Ndebele (Zimbabwe), Sebei (Uganda), Yoruba (Nigeria), Shona (Zimbabwe), Nupe (Nigeria), Illa (Zambia), and many others. There is, of course, a wide variation in understanding of the processes of rebirth: beliefs range from that in a "partial" reincarnation of an ancestor in one or several individuals strictly within the same family, to that in an endless cycle of rebirths linked to a notion of cleansing and refinement of the inner nature.
>
> As there are endless shades of understanding, reincarnation is known by many names: amongst the Yorubas of Nigeria rebirth is referred to in various ways, including Yiya omo, translated as the "shooting forth of a branch" or "turning to be child," and A-tun-wa, "another coming." The Aboh-speaking peoples of the Ibo family of nations in Nigeria speak of Inua u'we or "returning to life," as they believe death is an end to one life only and a gateway to another; man must be reborn, for reincarnation is a spiritual necessity.
>
> The ancient theosophy underlying traditional African religions becomes even more apparent as we delve into the fascinating complexities of their interpretations of the doctrine of rebirth.

29. Van Wyk, "African Traditional Religion," 704–5.

Appendix B

There seems to be a common belief amongst them that the wave of human souls at any particular world period is limited in number; therefore, reincarnation is only logical. For example, the Illa people of southern Zambia believe that a certain number of spirits were created and given bodies at the dawn of manifestation. When the bodies wear out during the course of a lifetime, the spirits live on in their own sphere of consciousness and then have other bodies prepared for them at the appropriate time. Linked with this is a belief in the inevitability of rebirth for the majority of humanity with only two exceptions cited by the Illa elders—the mizhimo or "tribal gods," and those unfortunate individuals whose spiritual evolution has in some way been interrupted by sorcerers. The Illa also believe that the reincarnating spirit is sexless and may seek manifestation in either the body of a man or woman regardless of the individual's sex in a previous life.[30]

9. Sikhism

Sikhism teaches that the soul reincarnates when the body dies. Sikhs do not believe in an afterlife that is either heaven or hell. . . .

A soul fortunate enough to achieve grace overcomes ego by meditating on God… The emancipated soul… exists eternally as an entity of radiant light.[31]

While Sikhs believe all souls will eventually achieve liberation, the religion also teaches that if a person does not perform righteous deeds, his/her soul will continue to be reincarnated.

People continue wandering through the cycle of 8.4 million incarnations; without the true Guru, liberation is not obtained. Reading and studying, the Pandits (religious scholars) and the silent sages have grown weary, but attached to the love of duality, they have lost their honor. The true Guru teaches the word of Shabad; without the True One, there is no other at all. Those who are linked by the True One are linked to Truth. They always act in Truth (Guru Granth Sahib Ji, 70).[32]

10. Juche ("Independent Stand" or "Self-Reliance")

30. Rooke, "Reincarnation in African Religion."
31. Khalsa, "Sikhism and the Afterlife."
32. RealSikhism, "Quotations > Reincarnation."

Juche is the only government-recognized ideology within North Korea. Not traditionally considered a religion, but more of a combination of philosophy, educational strategy, and religious practices, Juche could be described as a nationalist, secular, ethical ideology.[33]

The Juche religion does not advocate an official philosophy regarding life after death, or if there is such a thing. Therefore, no conclusion can be drawn regarding what its adherents believe will happen to them when they die. Research has revealed that some followers profess that, upon death, they will be reunited with Kim Il-Sung and be with him forever. This cannot be generalized as an accepted belief by all Juche followers. The afterlife is simply not the focus of the religion. Its foundational premise is that man is the master of everything and decides everything; so, whatever happens after death will be decided by man.

11. Spiritism (Also Referred to as Spiritualism)

The spiritualist's basic view of the afterlife is one where the dead are able to watch the living from a distance, and often want to offer advice to living friends and relatives about how to solve their earthly problems. They also offer encouragement to the living about the certainty of an afterlife that is largely pleasant and satisfying, and in doing so contradict claims about the extremes of heaven and hell described in mainstream Christianity.

Spiritualism can even be viewed as a concrete alternative to Christianity because the spirits purport to offer direct evidence of an afterlife by telling the audience facts about individuals in the audience that are unknown to the spiritualist and the rest of the audience. The target individual then confirms the facts to be correct and the audience concludes that the dead are indeed speaking. If the information is wrong or irrelevant (does not apply to the target individual), the spiritualist has various excuses about how or why the information got garbled.

The spiritualist's approach usually requires no faith in God or Christ though some churches wed the two very different systems of Christianity and Spiritualism in a strange admixture of often contradictory ideas (most spiritualists believe in reincarnation). There is also no need of attaining salvation to escape hell in the afterlife. [34]

33. Patheos, "Juche."
34. Denosky, "Spiritualism and Spiritual Travel."

Appendix B

Spiritualists are grounded in universal agreement that the soul of humans and potentially other living creatures live on after death.

> [Spiritualism] says that all people and animals that have been loved (had their vibrations raised) such as pets, continue to live after physical death. On crossing over we take three things with us: our etheric or spirit body (a duplicate of our physical body) all memories and our character.
>
> On crossing we go to a realm that will accommodate the vibrations we accumulated from all the thoughts and actions of our lifetime. Average decent people go to what is usually termed as the Third Realm. Those who have been willfully cruel and consistently selfish go to the darker, very unpleasant Astral regions because their level of vibrations would be much lower than the vibrations of the Third Realm.
>
> Information transmitted from the other side tells us that the Third Realm is a place of enormous beauty, peace and light. There will be scope to continue to spiritually refine indefinitely. Those who earned it can progress to the fourth level, then the fifth, and sixth and so on. For humans we know that there are at least seven realms vibrating from the lowest to the highest—the higher the vibrations the more beautiful and better the conditions. Spiritualists accept the Law of Progress—that those who are in the lower realms will one day slowly go upwardly towards the Realms of the Light even if it takes eons of time.[35]

While recognized as a major religion, Spiritualism is not organized in the same manner as more traditional religions.

> As an informal movement, Spiritualism does not have a defined set of rules, but various Spiritualist organizations have adopted variations on some or all of a 'Declaration of Principles' developed between 1899 and 1944 and revised as recently as 2004. In October 1899, a six article 'Declaration of Principles' was adopted by the National Spiritualist Association (NSA) at a convention in Chicago, Illinois. Two additional principles were added by the NSA in October 1909, at a convention in Rochester, New York. Finally, in October 1944, a ninth principle was adopted by the National Spiritualist Association of Churches, at a convention in St. Louis, Missouri.[36]

These nine principles set the foundation for Spiritualists beliefs.

---

35. Zammit, "Afterlife."
36. Wikipedia, "Spiritualism (Movement)."

The National Association of Spiritualist Churches in the USA has nine principles which provide more information about Spiritualist beliefs:

1. We believe in Infinite Intelligence.
2. We believe that the phenomena of Nature, both physical and spiritual, are the expression of Infinite Intelligence.
3. We affirm that a correct understanding of such expression and living in accordance therewith, constitute true religion.
4. We affirm that the existence and personal identity of the individual continue after the change called death.
5. We affirm that communication with the so-called dead is a fact, scientifically proven by the phenomena of Spiritualism.
6. We believe that the highest morality is contained in the Golden Rule: "Whatsoever ye would that others should do unto you do ye also unto them." ["Do unto others as you would have them do unto you."]
7. We affirm the moral responsibility of individuals and that we make our own happiness or unhappiness as we obey or disobey Nature's physical and spiritual laws.
8. We affirm that the doorway to reformation is never closed against any soul here or hereafter.
9. We affirm that the precepts of Prophecy and Healing are Divine attributes proven through Mediumship.[37]

These nine principles guide Spiritualists in their beliefs and relationship with God, while allowing each soul to achieve spiritual maturity in his/her own way.

> Spiritualism is too diverse to have a universal code of beliefs; instead, Spiritualists accept sets of more wide-ranging principles.
> ...
> The Spiritualists' National Union in the UK bases itself on the Seven Principles, which all full members must accept. These are:
>
> 1. The Fatherhood of God
> 2. The Brotherhood of Man
> 3. The Communion of Spirits and the Ministry of Angels
> 4. The continuous existence of the human soul
> 5. Personal responsibility

37. BBC, "Modern Spiritualism."

Appendix B

6. Compensation and retribution hereafter for all the good and evil deeds done on earth
7. Eternal progress open to every human soul[38]

12. Judaism

Beliefs about the afterlife and the fate of souls have varied throughout the life of Judaism.

> When examining Jewish intellectual sources throughout history, there is clearly a spectrum of opinions regarding death versus the afterlife....
>
> According to various Jewish intellectual sources and folk traditions up through the medieval period, there is a gradual transition from physical death to an afterlife in which the body and spirit remain connected to one another in some way either through resurrection or immortality of the soul....
>
> Finally, according to the rabbis, both the Jews and righteous Gentiles will receive salvation in olam ha-bah [the World to Come].[39]

While the continuation of the soul is a fundamental belief in Judaism, Jewish followers do not agree on the soul's fate.

> Traditional Judaism firmly believes that death is not the end of human existence. However, because Judaism is primarily focused on life here and now rather than on the afterlife, Judaism does not have much dogma about the afterlife, and leaves a great deal of room for one's personal opinion. It is possible for an Orthodox Jew to believe that the souls of the righteous dead go to a place similar to the Christian heaven, or that they are reincarnated through many lifetimes, or that they simply wait until the coming of the messiah, when they will be resurrected. Likewise, Orthodox Jews can believe that the souls of the wicked are tormented by demons of their own creation, or that wicked souls are simply destroyed at death, ceasing to exist.[40]

There is also no single agreement on the concept or the place called Hell within the Jewish community.

38. BBC, "Modern Spiritualism."
39. Patheos, "Judaism."
40. Zammit, "Afterlife."

Traditional Judaism teaches that after death our bodies go to the grave, but our souls go before God to be judged....

[S]ins that were not cleansed prior to death are removed after death in a place called Sheol or Gehinnom (also spelled Gehinom and Gehenna).

Contrary to the Christian view of eternal damnation in Hades or hell, the "punishment" of Sheol is temporary.

Just as all Christians do not agree on eschatology, all Jewish people do not agree on the afterlife. What the Bible clearly teaches is that sin demands a price to be paid by someone, there is an afterlife, and, in Christ, both Jews and Gentiles can have a place in Olam Ha-Ba, the World to Come.[41]

13. Bahá'í

The Bahá'í scriptures assert that there is life after death; indeed, the whole purpose of human life in this world is a preparation for that life....

[H]uman life in this world is like that of the embryo in the womb, which is developing arms, legs, eyes, and ears that are of little use in that world of the uterus. It is only when it dies to that world and is born into this world that it is able to use these organs fully....

There is no concept of a state of salvation in the Bahá'í teachings; rather salvation is a process. The process of acquiring spiritual virtues [kindness, generosity, integrity, truthfulness, humility, and selfless service to others] makes us more and more fit to enter the next world. The main aim of life should be to perfect these spiritual attributes; the more these are perfected, the closer humans become to God. And it is this closeness to God that is the heaven or paradise referred to in the scriptures of all religions. Failing to develop these virtues means humans separating themselves from God, and that is hell. Thus, heaven and hell are not distinct places; they are spiritual conditions both in this world and in the afterlife.[42]

14. Jainism

---

41. Got Questions, "Do Jews Believe in Hell?"
42. Patheos, "Bahá'í."

Appendix B

Karma—and its effect on human development—has a pivotal role in Jainism.

> In Jainism, godliness is said to be the inherent quality of every soul. This quality, however, is subdued by the soul's association with karmic matter. All souls who have achieved the natural state of infinite bliss, infinite knowledge (kevala jnana), infinite power and infinite perception are regarded as God in Jainism. Jainism rejects the idea of a creator deity responsible for the manifestation, creation, or maintenance of this universe. According to Jain doctrine, the universe and its constituents (soul, matter, space, time, and principles of motion) have always existed. All the constituents and actions are governed by universal natural laws and perfect soul, an immaterial entity cannot create or affect a material entity like the universe.[43]

Jains have a rather unique perspective on the human soul.

> Jain ideas about the soul differ from those of many other religions.
> The Jain word that comes closest to soul is *jiva*, which means a conscious, living being. For Jains body and soul are different things: the body is just an inanimate container—the conscious being is the jiva.
> After each bodily death, the jiva is reborn into a different body to live another life, until it achieves liberation. When a jiva is *embodied* (i.e., in a body), it exists throughout that body and isn't found in any particular bit of it.
> Jains believe:
> - the soul exists forever.
> - each soul is always independent.
> - the soul is responsible for what it does.
> - the soul experiences the consequences of its actions.
> - the soul can become liberated from the cycle of birth and death.
> - not all souls can be liberated—some souls are inherently incapable of achieving this.
> - the soul can evolve towards that liberation by following principles of behaviour.[44]

15. Shinto ("The Way of *Kami*" or "Way of the Gods")

43. Wikipedia, "God in Jainism."
44. BBC, "Jainism."

Winning with Your Body, Mind, and Soul

There is an old saying in Japan: 'born Shinto, die Buddhist.' Before Buddhism, it was believed that all who died went to a vast hellish underworld from which there is no escape. Buddhism introduced the idea of rewards and punishments in the afterlife, and death and salvation in the afterlife came to be regarded as Buddhist matters.[45]

Shinto focuses on this life rather than the next one.

Shinto is a difficult religion to classify. On the one hand, it can be seen as merely a highly sophisticated form of animism and may be regarded as a primal religion. On the other hand, Shinto beliefs and ways of thinking are deeply embedded in the subconscious fabric of modern Japanese society. The afterlife is not a primary concern in Shinto, and much more emphasis is placed on fitting into this world. . . . Shinto has no binding set of dogma, no holiest place for worshippers, no person or kami deemed holiest, and no defined set of prayers. Instead, Shinto is a collection of rituals and methods meant to mediate the relations of living humans to kami. . . .

[W]here Buddhism emphasizes the afterlife and ending the cycle of rebirths, Shinto emphasizes this life and finding happiness within it.[46]

Kami is a very important factor in Shinto.

Shinto traditions lean heavily on the concepts of the presence of kami and not reincarnation. The spiritual energy, or kami, in everyone is released and recycled at the time of death. The spirits live in another world, the most sacred of which is called "the other world of heaven." These other worlds are not seen as a paradise or a punishment. Instead the worlds are simply where the spirits reside. . . .

Shinto believes that the ancestral spirits will protect their descendants. The prayers and rituals performed by the living honor the dead and memorialize them. In return, the spirits of the dead offer protection and encouragement for the living.

Shintoism also views that some individuals live such an exemplary life that they become deified in a process called apotheosis. Many in the imperial family have experienced this honor, as have successful warriors.[47]

45. Patheos, "Shinto."
46. Yahoo! Answers, "Shintoism Belief about Afterlife?"
47. eCondolence, "Understanding Shinto."

Appendix B

Shinto views the spiritual energy in all living creatures as everlasting through its incorporation within kami. "There is no concept of an eternal soul in Shinto."[48]

16. Cao Dai ("Highest Lord" or "Highest Power")

> In Cao Dai, the purpose of life is peace within each individual and harmony in the world. Cao Dai followers . . . seek to gain religious merit and avoid bad karma.
>
> Cao Dai beliefs about the afterlife are derived from Buddhism. Those who have gathered too much bad karma . . . will be reincarnated in negative circumstances, which may include rebirth on a darker, colder planet. . . . Good karma leads to rebirth to a better life on earth.
>
> Salvation is freedom from rebirth and the attainment of nirvana or heaven. "The ultimate goal of Cao Daists is to be reunified with The All That Is, to return home."[49]

17. Zoroastrianism

> The Zoroastrian afterlife is determined by the balance of the good and evil deeds, words, and thoughts of the whole life. For those whose good deeds outweigh the bad, heaven awaits. Those who did more evil than good go to hell (which has several levels corresponding to degrees of wickedness). There is an intermediate stage for those whose deeds weight out equally.
>
> This general principle is not absolute, however, but allows for human weakness. All faults do not have to be registered or weighed forever on the scales. There are two means of effacing them: confession and the transfer of supererogatory merits (similar to the Roman Catholic "Treasury of Merits"). The latter is the basis for Zoroastrian prayers and ceremonies for the departed.[50]

The origins and dating of Zoroastrianism has been, and continues to be, debated among religious scholars.

> Consequently very influential ideas about the afterlife—like hell, heaven, individual judgment, resurrection of the dead, and last

---

48. Horton, "Shinto."
49. Religion Facts, "Cao Dai."
50. Religion Facts, "Zoroastrian Beliefs."

judgment—might originate here, or they might be later borrowings. We find the idea of the judgment of the individual at death as an element of the Egyptian afterlife, but there is no evidence of Egyptian influence on the ideas of Zoroastrianism. Zoroastrianism probably does introduce the idea of final judgment or Apocalypse (Frashegird or Frashokereti). The fate of wicked souls after the Frashgird evolved in Zoroastrianism. Scholars of Zoroastrianism find that in earlier texts, the souls would be subjected to everlasting punishment in hell, later the belief was that they would be destroyed in the molten metal of the Apocalypse, and even later belief holds that the molten metal will actually purify everything, allowing even the wicked to proceed to heaven. However, the ultimate fate of the wicked is not conclusively explained in any of the hell texts themselves.[51]

Research shows that Zoroastrian ideas regarding the nature of hell, and the fate of souls sent there, has changed throughout the life of the religion. And even from its earliest beginnings, there is evidence that these topics were not addressed conclusively.

> Even among Zoroastrian holy texts, you'll find only a few overt mentions of the nature of Hell, but the Book of Arda Viraf describes the Zoroastrian Hell as a place of fire with a terrible stench.... The Zoroastrian Hell... is not eternal and... God will purify all souls.[52]

18. Tenrikyō ("Religion of Divine Wisdom")

Tenrikyo affirms the concept of reincarnation, where the soul continually returns into the world with a new biological life after the death of the previous one. Reincarnation also appears in Indian religions such as Hinduism, Buddhism and Jainism.

Tenrikyo's understanding of reincarnation is referred to as *denaoshi* (出直し, "to make a fresh start"). *Denaoshi* is related to the teaching of a thing lent, a thing borrowed, in that when a person's physical body dies, the soul is returning to God the body that has been borrowed from God. This allows the soul to accept a new body to be lent by God and thus reenter the physical world. Though the reborn person has no memory of the previous life, the

---

51. Gardiner, "About Zoroastrian Hell."
52. Stuart, "Zoroastrians on Hell."

person's thoughts and deeds leave their mark on the soul and are carried over into the new life as the person's causality. . . .

Nakayama Miki taught that the process of *denaoshi* is like taking off old clothes in order to put on new ones, an image that emphasizes the materiality of the body. Human beings are given countless opportunities to realize the world of the Joyous Life (the state of salvation) in this world, as opposed to another realm in the afterlife such as heaven.[53]

Tenrikyō is primarily focused on achieving the best possible life here on earth.

The goal of Tenrikyō is a happy life free from disease and suffering. . . . The centre of religious activity is the *jiba*, a sacred recess in the sanctuary of the main temple in Tenri city (Nara Prefecture). The world is said to have been created here, and from the *jiba* salvation will finally be extended to the entire world.[54]

19. Neo-paganism

Neopaganism is not an organized religion and has no official doctrine. Pagans follow a wide variety of paths and may have a variety of beliefs on religious questions like the divine, human nature and the afterlife. However, there are some common beliefs that are held by most Neopagans.[55]

The common portrayal of the Summerland is as a place of rest for souls in between their earthly incarnations.

In Theosophy, the term "Summerland" is used without the definite article "the." Summerland, also called the Astral plane Heaven, is depicted as where souls who have been good in their previous lives go between incarnations. . . .

The final permanent eternal afterlife heaven to which Theosophists believe most people will go millions or billions of years in the future, after our cycle of reincarnations in this Round is over, is called Nirvana, and is located beyond this physical Cosmos.[56]

---

53. Wikipedia, "Tenrikyo Anthropology."
54. Encyclopedia Britannica, "Tenrikyō."
55. Religion Facts, "Neopagan Beliefs."
56. Wikipedia, "The Summerland."

Research reveals a range of beliefs among neo-pagans regarding the afterlife. Below are some results based on questions in a Belief-O-Matic quiz.

> Many believe in reincarnation after some rest and recovery in the 'Otherworld.' There is generally no concept of hell as a place of punishment. . . . Some (Wicca) believe the soul joins their dead ancestors. . . . Some believe that life energy continues in some, if unknown, form. Some believe in various spiritual resting places. Many say we don't or can't know what happens after death.[57]

20. Unitarian Universalism

Unitarian Universalism (UU) is a liberal religion characterized by a "free and responsible search for truth and meaning." Unitarian Universalists assert no creed, but instead are unified by their shared search for spiritual growth, guided by a dynamic, "living tradition." Currently, these traditions are summarized by the Six Sources and Seven Principles of Unitarian Universalism, documents recognized by all congregations who choose to be a part of the Unitarian Universalist Association. These documents are "living," meaning always open for revisiting and reworking. Unitarian Universalist (U.U.) congregations include many atheists, agnostics, and theists within their membership—and there are U.U. churches, fellowships, congregations, and societies all over America—as well as others around the world. The roots of Unitarian Universalism lie in liberal Christianity, specifically Unitarianism and universalism. Unitarian Universalists state that from these traditions comes a deep regard for intellectual freedom and inclusive love. Congregations and members seek inspiration and derive insight from all major world religions.

The beliefs of individual Unitarian Universalists range widely, including atheism, agnosticism, pantheism, panentheism, pandeism, deism, humanism, Judaism, Christianity, Islam, Hinduism, Sikhism, Buddhism, Taoism, syncretism, Omnism, Neopaganism and the teachings of the Bahá'í Faith.

The Unitarian Universalist Association (UUA) was formed in 1961 through the consolidation of the American Unitarian Association, established in 1825, and the Universalist Church of America, established in 1793. The UUA is headquartered in Boston, Massachusetts, and serves churches mostly in the United

---

57. Beliefnet, "What Neo-pagans Believe."

Appendix B

States. A group of thirty Philippine congregations is represented as a sole member within the UUA. The Canadian Unitarian Council (CUC) became an independent body in 2002. The UUA and CUC are, in turn, two of the seventeen members of the International Council of Unitarians and Universalists.[58]

Like several other religions, Unitarian Universalists have a broad set of beliefs regarding the afterlife.

> While there are a variety of views of the afterlife, most Unitarian Universalists consider this life the important one. Some believe in an ultimate unification with God, or the universe. Many Unitarian Universalists believe that the only afterlife is the legacy people leave on earth. . . . [H]ell is rarely discussed except as a metaphor. . . . Salvation receives little attention.[59]

Unitarian Universalism grew out of Christianity.

> Christian universalism is a school of Christian theology focused around the doctrine of universal reconciliation—the view that all human beings will ultimately be "saved" and restored to a right relationship with God. Christian universalism and the belief or hope in the universal reconciliation through Christ can even be understood as synonyms.
>
> The term Christian universalism was used in the 1820s by Russell Streeter of the *Christian Intelligencer* of Portland—a descendant of Adams Streeter who had founded one of the first Universalist Churches on September 14, 1785. Christian universalists believe this was the most common interpretation of Christianity in Early Christianity, prior to the 6th century. Christians from a diversity of denominations and traditions believe in the tenets of Christian universalism, such as the reality of an afterlife without the possibility of eternal punishment in hell.
>
> As a formal Christian denomination, Christian universalism originated in the late 18th century with the Universalist Church of America. There is currently no single denomination uniting Christian universalists, but a few denominations teach some of the principles of Christian universalism or are open to them. In 2007, the Christian Universalist Association was founded to serve as an ecumenical umbrella organization for churches, ministries, and individuals who believe in Christian universalism.

---

58. Wikipedia, "Unitarian Universalism."
59. Unitarian Universalist Association, "Leader Resource 3."

Unitarian Universalism historically grew out of Christian universalism but is not an exclusively Christian denomination. It formed from a 1961 merger of two historically Christian denominations, the Universalist Church of America and the American Unitarian Association, both based in the United States.[60]

21. Rastafarianism

Rastafari has been characterized as a millenarianist movement, for it espouses the idea that the present age will come to an apocalyptic end. With Babylon destroyed, Rastas believe that humanity will be ushered into a "new age." In the 1980s, Rastas believed that this would happen around the year 2000. In this Day of Judgement, Babylon will be overthrown, and Rastas would be the chosen few who survive. A common view in the Rasta community was that the world's white people would wipe themselves out through nuclear war, with black Africans then ruling the world, something that they argue is prophesied in Daniel 2:31–32. In Rasta belief, the end of this present age would be followed by a millennium of peace, justice, and happiness in Ethiopia. The righteous will live in paradise in Africa. Those who had supported Babylon will be denied access to paradise. The Rasta conception of salvation has similarities with that promoted in Judaism.

Rastas do not believe that there is a specific afterlife to which human individuals go following bodily death. They believe in the possibility of eternal life, and that only those who shun righteousness will actually die. One Rasta view is that those who are righteous are believed to go through a process of reincarnation, with an individual's identity remaining throughout each of their incarnations. Barrett observed some Jamaican Rastas who believed that those Rastas who did die had not been faithful to Jah (God). He suggested that this attitude stemmed from the large numbers of young people that were then members of the movement, and who had thus seen only few Rastas die. In keeping with their views on death, Rastas eschew celebrating physical death and often avoid funerals, also repudiating the practice of ancestor veneration that is common among African traditional religions.[61]

Rastafarianism does not support the idea of any other worlds, realms, or dimensions besides the physical or natural world.

60. Wikipedia, "Christian Universalism."
61. Wikipedia, "Rastafari."

Appendix B

Ethiopia, specifically, Africa in general, is considered the Rastas' heaven on earth. There is no afterlife or hell as Christianity believes. Rastas believe that Jah will send the signal and help the blacks exodus back to [Ethiopia], their homeland. Any news from Ethiopia was taken very seriously as a warning to get ready to leave. The belief stems from Marcus Garvey's theme, 'Back to Africa.' Although Selassie's death came before this was possible, it did succeed in turning blacks desire to look towards Africa as their roots.[62]

Physical immortality is a foundational belief in Rastafarianism.

True Rastas are believed to be immortal, both physically and spiritually, a concept called "ever living." In keeping with a philosophy that celebrates life, many Rastafarians deny the possibility of death, except as a consequence of sin, and believe that the doctrine of the existence of, and reward in, the afterlife is the White man's teaching aimed at deflecting Blacks from the pursuit of their just rewards in this life. "We believe in Jesus but not the Jesus that you have to know to go to Heaven or Hell.... We see Jesus more for the things that he taught," says Knight, "instead of focusing on Heaven or Hell as your salvation."[63]

22. Scientology

For Scientologists, the true self is the spirit, the thetan, the eternal essence of each individual. For millions and millions of years prior to this life, the thetan has existed and inhabited numerous bodies. This process of moving on and being reborn as a baby in a new body, called reincarnation or rebirth in some eastern religions, occurs as a natural and normal part of the universe.... At the same time, it also differs in important respects from eastern ideas. For example, there is no belief in karma nor is the thetan seen as experiencing any kind of moral judgment between lives that has any role in determining its next incarnation. Also, Scientologists reject any notion that a thetan would be reincarnated as an animal or in any state less than human.[64]

---

62. Meta Religion, "The Rastafarian Religion."
63. FindYourFate.com, "Rastafari."
64. Patheos, "Scientology."

Appendix C

Probability of Achieving Your Desire—Avoiding a Bad Afterlife—with Each Major Religion

Afterlife Possibility	Entity Determining the Outcome	Outcome	Religion with Unique or Additional Requirement	Christianity	Islam	Non-religious	Hinduism
Without a Trace							
				1.00	1.00	1.00	1.00
Déjà Vu							
	Individual			0.50	0.50	0.50	0.50
The Merry-Go-Round							
Ain't No Stopping Us Now		No Escape		1.00	1.00	1.00	1.00
Reunited, and It Feels So Good	Individual	Reunion		1.00	1.00	1.00	1.00
Eraser	God/ Individual	Reunion/ Destroyed		1.00	1.00	1.00	1.00
Judgment Day							
Control	Individual	Close to God		0.50	0.50	0.50	0.50
The Scales of Justice	God						
Purified		Purified		1.00	1.00	0.00	1.00
Destroyed		Destroyed		1.00	1.00	0.00	1.00
Punished		Heaven					
			Islam	0.00	0.50	0.00	0.00

Appendix C

			African Traditional and Diasporic	0.50	0.50	0.00	0.50
			Judaism	0.50	0.50	0.00	0.50
The Lion and the Lamb	Jesus Christ		Christianity	1.00	0.00	0.00	0.00
Decision Day							
	Individual			1.00	1.00	1.00	1.00
Overall Probability				0.7692	0.7308	0.4615	0.6923
*Note:	Scoring is for those groups within the religion that ascribe to a final judgment with the possibility of eternal punishment. Other afterlife possibilities include no heaven and no hell (scored under Déjà Vu) and endless reincarnation (scored under The Merry-Go-Round: Ain't No Stopping Us Now).						
**Note:	Scoring is for traditional Unitarian Universalists who accept the doctrine of universal reconciliation. Adherents who have adopted the beliefs of other faiths would receive the scores of those specific religions.						

Winning with Your Body, Mind, and Soul

Afterlife Possibility	Entity Determining the Outcome	Outcome	Religion with Unique or Additional Requirement	Chinese Traditional			Buddhism
				Taoism	Confucianism	Folk-Religionist	
Without a Trace							
				1.00	1.00	1.00	1.00
Déjà Vu							
	Individual			0.50	0.50	0.50	0.50
The Merry-Go-Round							
Ain't No Stopping Us Now		No Escape		1.00	1.00	1.00	1.00
Reunited, and It Feels So Good	Individual	Reunion		1.00	1.00	1.00	1.00
Eraser	God/Individual	Reunion/Destroyed		1.00	1.00	1.00	1.00
Judgment Day							
Control	Individual	Close to God		0.50	0.50	0.50	0.50
The Scales of Justice	God						
Purified		Purified		0.00	0.00	1.00	0.00
Destroyed		Destroyed		0.00	0.00	1.00	0.00
Punished		Heaven					
			Islam	0.00	0.00	0.00	0.00
			African Traditional and Diasporic	0.00	0.00	0.50	0.00
			Judaism	0.00	0.00	0.50	0.00
The Lion and the Lamb	Jesus Christ		Christianity	0.00	0.00	0.00	0.00
Decision Day							
	Individual			1.00	1.00	1.00	1.00
Overall Probability				0.4615	0.4615	0.6923	0.4615

Appendix C

*Note:	Scoring is for those groups within the religion that ascribe to a final judgment with the possibility of eternal punishment. Other afterlife possibilities include no heaven and no hell (scored under Déjà Vu) and endless reincarnation (scored under The Merry-Go-Round: Ain't No Stopping Us Now).				
**Note:	Scoring is for traditional Unitarian Universalists who accept the doctrine of universal reconciliation. Adherents who have adopted the beliefs of other faiths would receive the scores of those specific religions.				

Winning with Your Body, Mind, and Soul

Afterlife Possibility	Entity Determining the Outcome	Outcome	Religion with Unique or Additional Requirement	Primal-Indigenous			Animist	Shamanist
				Ethno-religionist				
				Christianity-Based	Islam-Based	Buddhism-Based		
Without a Trace								
				1.00	1.00	1.00	1.00	1.00
Déjà Vu								
		Individual		0.50	0.50	0.50	0.50	0.50
The Merry-Go-Round								
Ain't No Stopping Us Now		No Escape		1.00	1.00	1.00	1.00	1.00
Reunited, and It Feels So Good	Individual	Reunion		1.00	1.00	1.00	1.00	1.00
Eraser	God/Individual	Reunion/Destroyed		1.00	1.00	1.00	1.00	1.00
Judgment Day								
Control	Individual	Close to God		0.50	0.50	0.50	0.50	0.50
The Scales of Justice	God							
Purified		Purified		1.00	1.00	0.00	0.00	0.00
Destroyed		Destroyed		1.00	1.00	0.00	0.00	0.00
Punished		Heaven						
			Islam	0.00	0.50	0.00	0.00	0.00
			African Traditional and Diasporic	0.50	0.50	0.00	0.00	0.00
			Judaism	0.50	0.50	0.00	0.00	0.00
The Lion and the Lamb	Jesus Christ		Christianity	1.00	0.00	0.00	0.00	0.00
Decision Day								
	Individual			1.00	1.00	1.00	1.00	1.00

Appendix C

				0.7692	0.7308	0.4615	0.4615	0.4615
Overall Probability								
*Note:	Scoring is for those groups within the religion that ascribe to a final judgment with the possibility of eternal punishment. Other afterlife possibilities include no heaven and no hell (scored under Déjà Vu) and endless reincarnation (scored under The Merry-Go-Round: Ain't No Stopping Us Now).								
**Note:	Scoring is for traditional Unitarian Universalists who accept the doctrine of universal reconciliation. Adherents who have adopted the beliefs of other faiths would receive the scores of those specific religions.								

Afterlife Possibility	Entity Determining the Outcome	Outcome	Religion with Unique or Additional Requirement	African Traditional and Diasporic*	Sikhism	Juche	Spiritism	Judaism
Without a Trace								
				1.00	1.00	1.00	1.00	1.00
Déjà Vu								
	Individual			0.50	0.50	0.50	0.50	0.50
The Merry-Go-Round								
Ain't No Stopping Us Now		No Escape		1.00	1.00	1.00	1.00	1.00
Reunited, and It Feels So Good	Individual	Reunion		1.00	1.00	1.00	1.00	1.00
Eraser	God/Individual	Reunion/Destroyed		1.00	1.00	1.00	1.00	1.00
Judgment Day								
Control	Individual	Close to God		0.50	0.50	0.50	0.50	0.50
The Scales of Justice	God							
Purified		Purified		1.00	1.00	0.00	1.00	1.00
Destroyed		Destroyed		1.00	1.00	0.00	1.00	1.00
Punished		Heaven						
			Islam	0.00	0.50	0.00	0.50	0.50
			African Traditional and Diasporic	0.50	0.50	0.00	0.50	0.50
			Judaism	0.50	0.50	0.00	0.50	0.50
The Lion and the Lamb	Jesus Christ		Christianity	0.00	0.00	0.00	0.00	0.00
Decision Day								
	Individual			1.00	1.00	1.00	1.00	1.00
Overall Probability				0.6923	0.7308	0.4615	0.7308	0.7308

Appendix C

*Note:	Scoring is for those groups within the religion that ascribe to a final judgment with the possibility of eternal punishment. Other afterlife possibilities include no heaven and no hell (scored under Déjà Vu) and endless reincarnation (scored under The Merry-Go-Round: Ain't No Stopping Us Now).					
**Note:	Scoring is for traditional Unitarian Universalists who accept the doctrine of universal reconciliation. Adherents who have adopted the beliefs of other faiths would receive the scores of those specific religions.					

Winning with Your Body, Mind, and Soul

Afterlife Possibility	Entity Determining the Outcome	Outcome	Religion with Unique or Additional Requirement	Bahá'í	Jainism	Shinto	Cao Dai	Zoroastrianism
Without a Trace								
				1.00	1.00	1.00	1.00	1.00
Déjà Vu								
	Individual			0.50	0.50	0.50	0.50	0.50
The Merry-Go-Round								
Ain't No Stopping Us Now		No Escape		1.00	1.00	1.00	1.00	1.00
Reunited, and It Feels So Good	Individual	Reunion		1.00	1.00	1.00	1.00	1.00
Eraser	God/ Individual	Reunion/ Destroyed		1.00	1.00	1.00	1.00	1.00
Judgment Day								
Control	Individual	Close to God		0.50	0.50	0.50	0.50	0.50
The Scales of Justice	God							
Purified		Purified		1.00	0.00	0.00	1.00	1.00
Destroyed		Destroyed		1.00	0.00	0.00	1.00	1.00
Punished		Heaven						
			Islam	0.50	0.00	0.00	0.00	0.50
			African Traditional and Diasporic	0.50	0.00	0.00	0.50	0.50
			Judaism	0.50	0.00	0.00	0.50	0.50
The Lion and the Lamb	Jesus Christ		Christianity	0.00	0.00	0.00	0.00	0.00
Decision Day								
	Individual			1.00	1.00	1.00	1.00	1.00
Overall Probability				0.7308	0.4615	0.4615	0.6923	0.7308

Appendix C

*Note:	Scoring is for those groups within the religion that ascribe to a final judgment with the possibility of eternal punishment. Other afterlife possibilities include no heaven and no hell (scored under Déjà Vu) and endless reincarnation (scored under The Merry-Go-Round: Ain't No Stopping Us Now).					
**Note:	Scoring is for traditional Unitarian Universalists who accept the doctrine of universal reconciliation. Adherents who have adopted the beliefs of other faiths would receive the scores of those specific religions.					

Winning with Your Body, Mind, and Soul

Afterlife Possibility	Entity Determining the Outcome	Outcome	Religion with Unique or Additional Requirement	Tenrikyo	Neo-paganism	Unitarian Universalism**	Rastafarianism	Scientology
Without a Trace								
				1.00	1.00	1.00	1.00	1.00
Déjà Vu								
	Individual			0.50	0.50	0.50	0.50	0.50
The Merry-Go-Round								
Ain't No Stopping Us Now		No Escape		1.00	1.00	1.00	1.00	1.00
Reunited, and It Feels So Good	Individual	Reunion		1.00	1.00	1.00	1.00	1.00
Eraser	God/ Individual	Reunion/ Destroyed		1.00	1.00	1.00	1.00	1.00
Judgment Day								
Control	Individual	Close to God		0.50	0.50	0.50	0.50	0.50
The Scales of Justice	God							
Purified		Purified		1.00	0.00	1.00	1.00	1.00
Destroyed		Destroyed		1.00	0.00	1.00	1.00	1.00
Punished		Heaven						
			Islam	0.50	0.00	0.50	0.50	0.50
			African Traditional and Diasporic	0.50	0.00	0.50	0.50	0.50
			Judaism	0.50	0.00	0.50	0.50	0.50
The Lion and the Lamb	Jesus Christ		Christianity	0.00	0.00	0.00	0.00	0.00
Decision Day								

Appendix C

	Individual			1.00	1.00	1.00	1.00	1.00
Overall Probability				0.7308	0.4615	0.7308	0.7308	0.7308
*Note:	Scoring is for those groups within the religion that ascribe to a final judgment with the possibility of eternal punishment. Other afterlife possibilities include no heaven and no hell (scored under Déjà Vu) and endless reincarnation (scored under The Merry-Go-Round: Ain't No Stopping Us Now).							
**Note:	Scoring is for traditional Unitarian Universalists who accept the doctrine of universal reconciliation. Adherents who have adopted the beliefs of other faiths would receive the scores of those specific religions.							

About the Author

Henry Arnold Davis is the author of *Gambling With Your Soul: What Is Your Best Bet?* and the vice president of quality assurance with Armorworks Enterprises in Chandler, Arizona. Henry holds degrees in electrical engineering and business administration from Yale University and the Stanford Graduate School of Business respectively. He has been a business owner and held leadership positions at several Fortune 500 companies in the aerospace and automotive industries. He has traveled extensively throughout the world, visiting and/or conducting business in more than twenty-five countries and territories on four continents. Henry lives in Chandler, Arizona, with his wife of twenty-four years, Tanya, enjoying the Valley of the Sun. Combined, they have five children and twelve grandchildren.

Appendix C

Other Titles from Henry Arnold Davis
Gambling With Your Soul: What Is Your Best Bet?
Website: www.henryarnolddavis.com

If you've ever wondered "What will happen to me when I die?" this book is for you. I first considered the question at eight years of age staring down the barrel of a thirty-eight-caliber revolver under a white-knuckled death grip in my father's hand—the same gun used on him by my older brother years earlier. Drawing on religion, science, philosophy, mathematics, near-death experiences (NDE), out-of-body experiences (OBE), spirit encounters, hundreds of interviews across the globe, and good old-fashioned common sense, *Gambling With Your Soul* tackles the controversial topic of life after death by standing on two fundamental truths. First, everyone is going to die. Second, no one knows what will happen to them after they die. In the face of these truths, *What Is Your Best Bet?* Analyzing the afterlife beliefs of the world's top twenty-two religions/nonreligions, this book proves it is Christianity. This is not to say that Christianity is "right," and all other religions are "wrong." It is simply your best bet. The book provides an original, objective, and comprehensive answer to the question that's sewn into the DNA of every human being.

"In *Gambling With Your Soul*, Henry Arnold Davis offers a multi-faceted and multi-disciplinary approach to how one thinks about living and the afterlife. Davis' powerful personal narrative intersects with his knowledge of religions around the world to capture any reader regardless of religious or faith beliefs. Highly recommended!"
  —Dr. Russell Wigginton, President, National Civil Rights Museum
    Author of *The Strange Career of the Black Athlete*

"Henry Arnold Davis takes a provoking, personal look at human death in *Gambling With Your Soul*. He gradually and eloquently explores the possibility of life after death through stories, personal experiences, and interreligious views. *Gambling With Your Soul* is a thought-provoking page-turner!"
  —Reverend Dr. Humberto Alfaro, Professor of Practical Theology
    Director of the Center for Pentecostal Leadership
    New York Theological Seminary

"Exploring the question of what happens after we die, *Gambling With Your Soul* analyzes the world's top religions and non-religions to find the best bet for a meaningful afterlife. Stimulating, thorough, and thought-provoking."
  —Christina Baker Kline, #1 New York Times bestselling author
    of eight novels, including *The Exiles*, *Orphan Train* and
    A Piece of the World

"Henry Arnold Davis in *Gambling With Your Soul* offers us a detailed and careful apologia for Jesus as the only true savior of the world. He has a rich understanding of various world religions, and what they teach about the afterlife. He also provides richly competent treatments of near-death experiences. Using the logic of the engineer and business executive that he is, he makes a meticulous case for why one's best bet for a safe and secure afterlife is faith in Jesus as the savior while in this life. I heartily recommend this carefully reasoned and thoughtful book!"
  —Dr. David C. Asomaning, author of *Nightmares to Miracles* and
    Signs and Wonders
    SynchroMind®: The Leadership Development Company

"My daughter and I attended Henry's book signing shortly after she had completed her first book simply to get an idea of what a book signing was

Appendix C

supposed to be. What we took away from that was much more than either of us could have pictured. *Gambling With Your Soul* has been a great tool for us to talk together about God, some of the questions faith can bring, and what happens next. Recently her 10th grade class had experienced an accidental death as well as a suicide and that left her with many questions. Henry's detailed and analytical approach to this age-old question provided me and my daughter many nights of quality time discussing how different views are always optional, but that in the end your faith in God is the best option available. Henry Arnold Davis is a remarkable writer with an educational background that far surpasses most, but his ability to capture audiences from all age levels as well as diverse faiths made this an extraordinary read and experience with my family."

—John and Ella Lybarger, author of *Loud Thoughts* and *Opposite Thoughts*

"The best part of reading *Gambling With Your Soul* was feeling like Henry Arnold Davis was walking alongside me . . . as I delved into my own personal childhood trauma. I was triggered and also comforted by his story, knowing that I was not alone and that I could survive this courageous journey. I wholeheartedly endorse this amazing book!"

—Reverend Dr. Nadja Fidelia, former Managing Director, Lehman Brothers, Co-Founder of Eland Capital Partners

"A fascinating read from beginning to end. If you've ever asked yourself life's most profound question—What will happen to me when I die?—this book is for you. The author grabbed my attention with a bang and held it firmly with interesting stories and thought-provoking questions. A must read!"

—John Ortiz, California, no religious affiliation

"Recommend for readers who enjoy a serious study of various religious beliefs and seek to find the true God. Through stories, history, personal experiences, various research, and reflections, the reader is guided from an objective perspective to consider a true belief."

—Christina Tse, Hong Kong, converted from pantheism to Christianity

"The feeling of confronting death is lonely and overwhelming and has deep impact on a person. This book works on easing that experience by showing that death is universal. This exposure to the universality of death can have an emotional relief leading to faster acceptance."
—Salem Wali Ali, California, Muslim

www.ingramcontent.com/pod-product-compliance
Lightning Source LLC
Chambersburg PA
CBHW051057160426
43193CB00010B/1225